THE

AMBASSADOR

OF

GOD

'Occasionally, a man stumbles over the truth. Most dust themselves off and continue walking as though nothing had happened'.

– Winston Churchill

INTRODUCTION: THE UNIVERSE OR GOD?

In my quiet pursuits, I discovered a quotation from Albert Einstein that has served me well – *Any fool can know. The point is to understand.*

To depersonalise and objectify 'God' as an 'infinite nothingness' and a metonym for 'the universe' has become a custom for many in our society. In an attempt to make sense of it all, some have adopted this vague ideology and view in understanding God by substituting the creator God with a created universe.

Perhaps, it is time to undress this obscurity and inspect its private parts. If those who uphold such views are 'absolutely' certain of their intellectual position and beliefs, they should also take the time to teach us what the universe absolutely is. Sadly, none of them have done this. However, many blindly embrace and follow their derision.

3

It is pretentious to appoint 'the universe' as a dogma and a central theme in promoting our ideologies and philosophies if we do not possess universal knowledge! Till this day, over 95% of the universe is admittedly unknown to astrophysicists, and we are still discovering new information about the remaining 4 - 5% of the universe. Evidently, more is unknown than known about our universe.

There is nothing wrong in being a poet, a wordsmith, and flirting with words if that is what we do and what we say we are, but to pose as 'messengers of light' and hide ambiguity behind esoteric scientific terminologies is misleading and intellectually dishonest. Before employing a big word like 'the universe' as a theme in our doctrinal teachings, we should try to define 'the universe' to our audience in a literal and factual context so they can better understand what it is we are saying and where we are coming from. Better still; let's start by defining and conjoining the astrophysical knowledge of one of our neighbouring solar planets like Mars or Jupiter in correlation to our spiritual ideologies and philosophies. For if we cannot make an example of a solar system planet that is near by, how can we possibly understand the extra solar planetary systems that exist in the far regions of the universe?

When we use buzz words like 'the universe' to communicate with the masses without a thorough explanation and understanding of what the universe is, we deceive ourselves and others. Masquerading 'the universe' as a term to fit our philosophical models without a correspondent evidential basis is an imitation of science – an unsubstantiated conjecture, alternatively known as Pseudoscience.

Why do we use words and terms the public do not entirely understand, to influence and control the things that they do know? Why do we use words that have defined and clear meanings ambiguously or choose to trifle and alter well known dictionary words duplicitously? Even invisible entities and persons like angels have specific descriptions and names so why do we choose to use the universe in an obscure and vague manner? Sadly, we have encouraged obscurity to create a false sense of freedom. The public deserve so much more.

DEDICATION

I dedicate this book to the Father, the Son and the Holy Ghost

I don't know where to start. I don't have the words to thank you enough for everything - the past, the present and the future, Lord you know, Lord you know but if I may for all time speak this once, and forever be silent and forgotten.

Can I just say?

You are my earth, you keep me from falling. You are my moon; you keep me safe and warm. You are my sun; you brighten my day with love and compassion. You are my star: you're the reason I live, the reason I am, the reason I write. You're my everything.

Published by Mahc Jizm Ltd

978-0-9566404-3-7 (Limited Edition Hardback)

978-0-9566404-6-8 (Limited Edition Paperback)

Scripture quotations are taken from the King James Version of the Bible unless otherwise noted.

Scripture quotations are also taken from the New King James Version. © 1982 Thomas Nelson, Inc. Used by permission. All rights reserved.

Contents

PREFACE

When I think of God, I think of our entire globe and planet.

I think of the **MOON** and **SUN**. I think of other planets as well - like Mars, Mercury and Jupiter.

I think of the vast cosmos of **STARS** and black holes.

I think of rain and <u>**WATER**</u>; light, thunder, and energy, I think of everything.

<u>I think of you and I</u>, how small we are (?), how fragile and frail (?) living on a small isolated planet in the cosmic sea of galaxies and space. I think of how alone and lost we may feel...

I think of the pre-scientific books we were given – the TORAH, BIBLE and QURAN.

What could they possibly tell me about God?

What could they possibly reveal about THE CREATOR of everything? What are their views on our cosmic origin and beginning?

How could a Rabbi in Israel claim to be the <u>biological son of GOD</u>? What possible kinship could he have with the extraordinary cosmos? Who are prophets and messengers of GOD?

What's the BIG PICTURE? What's the meaning of it all? Who or what is **GOD**?

When I think of God, I think about everything. I mean... **<u>EVERYTHING</u>!**

VOLUME 2

THE SUN, THE MOON... AND THE STARS

'The heavens declare the glory of God; and the firmament shows His handiwork. Day unto day [sun] *utters speech, and night unto night* [moon and stars] *reveals knowledge. There is no speech nor language* [nations of people] *where their voice is not heard. Their line has gone out through the earth, and their words to the end of the world...*

~ Psalms 19: 1-4

I was sleeping all alone in my room when a loud whisper woke me up *Count the years between you and your brother, Isaac,* the voice said. *I am sending you to the whole world, to the four corners of the earth* | + |, *to both male and female from this flat that you are living in, just like the distance from the sun to the earth.*

13

To my astonishment, I later discovered the distance between the sun and the earth was exactly 93 million miles and I lived at number 93... in London. I also grew up in a family of six: two parents (one woman and one man) and four siblings (two girls and two boys).

I have an older sister who is three years older than me, a younger sister who is three years younger than me, and my brother Isaac is three years younger than my second sister, which makes Isaac six years younger than me.

I had learned from Bible numerology that the number six symbolised earth and humanity because God had made both man and woman on the sixth day, and had made the earth in six days before he chose to rest on the seventh. So the words I had heard from the voice coincided harmoniously: *I am sending you to the whole world, to the four corners of the earth, to both male and female from this flat that you are living in, just like the distance from the sun to the earth.*

The most brilliant scientists in modern history were those who spoke Biblical truths intentionally or unwittingly. I am no scientist – all I've ever known, which I learned as a child, is the Bible. I did not realise I had learnt anything more...

Recorded for us in the gospels of Matthew and Mark are two Biblical narratives that are pivotal to the context for which this volume was written. I have included these scriptures in full (and other corresponding scriptures in this volume) because it is necessary to do so for our comparative study of astronomy and the Bible.

In Matthew 12:38–40, the scripture narrates: *Then some of the scribes and Pharisees asked, saying, "Teacher, we want to see a sign from You." But He answered and said to them, "An evil and adulterous generation seeks after a sign, and no sign will be given to it except the sign of the prophet Jonah. For as Jonah was three days and three nights in the belly of the great fish, so will the Son of Man be three days and three nights in the heart of the earth.*

And Mark 8:11–12 states: *Then the Pharisees came out and began to dispute with Him, seeking from Him a sign from heaven, testing Him. But He sighed deeply in His spirit, and said, 'Why does this generation seek a sign? Assuredly, I say to you, no sign shall be given to this generation.'*

Evidently, as we find in the scriptures, the Pharisees and Sadducees had many questions for Jesus, and Jesus often answered their questions with more questions. Though these men asked for a sign from heaven (i.e. the cosmos), they barely understood astronomy in their days. Arguably, few were acquainted with astrology. Assuming Jesus had given them a sign (a clue) that revealed the hidden activities of the cosmos, their limited knowledge of science could not have helped to validate the authenticity of such sign(s) or divine revelation. Though the potential for modern technology in astronomy had been present on earth from primitive times, the generation at the time of Christ Jesus had not yet advanced in knowledge to astrophysics and astrodynamics. They vaguely understood cosmology and knew very little of astrogeometry, so their questioning was pretentious. This is why Jesus preferred to use analogies and metaphors within their scope of knowledge and understanding.

Assuming it was this generation that asked Jesus the same question(s) about the cosmos, the prospects of answering such questions favourably may have been advantageous for Jesus and this generation, because this present generation have the scientific knowledge and tools to examine the activities in the cosmos. Considering astronomy or even astrology was not a profession of the scribes and Pharisees, how could they possibly appreciate a revelatory dialogue with Jesus about the cosmos? Instead of sharing information that they were not familiar with, Jesus ignored their cunning pretences by sharing a revelation that is simple and relevant to their education history. They were scholars of the scriptures, so Jesus used the narrative of the Prophet Jonah to illustrate his divine assignment on earth, which was his death (1), his burial (2) and his resurrection (3). Jesus also left them a clue – the number three.

In our planetary system, it has been confirmed by scientists that the planet Earth is the third planet from the Sun. Though planets Mercury and Venus, closer to the Sun than planet Earth, are also described as terrestrial and earth-like by astronomers, life for some odd reason(s) began on the third planet!

Furthermore, in the story of creation from Genesis 1:13–16, the scripture categorised the celestial lights in the heavens into three: the sun, the moon and the stars. But what was the reason for this classification, and in what order of significance were these lights created? Let's turn to Genesis 1:13–16 to review:

*So the evening and the morning were the third day. Then God said, 'Let there be lights in the firmament of the heavens to divide the day from the night; and let them be for **signs**, and seasons, and for days* *and years; and let them be for lights in the firmament of the heavens to give light on the earth'; and it was so. Then God made two great lights: the greater light* [sun] *to rule the day, and the lesser light* [moon] *to rule the night. He made the stars also.*

According to this passage of scripture, the primary intention for the creation of the celestial lights was for 'signs', and the second, third and fourth reasons were for seasons, days and years. If we examine these scripture verses closely, we will find that the primary intention for their creation does not belong in the same category as the others. While the second, third and fourth purpose for their creation points to an earthly use, the first purpose for their existence as 'signs' points to a heavenly cause and assignment. This would mean that the sun, moon and stars may contain inherent empirical information and behavioural patterns within their astrophysical bodies that point to the supernatural.

Undoubtedly and most certainly, if it is that the Biblical God is the creator of these celestial bodies of lights, it should be of no surprise to find that the astrophysical knowledge of the celestial lights point to the Biblical account of their creator.

As 'signs', the representation of the sun, moon and stars is essentially analogous with the triune deity, as there is no other biblical subject more objective than the Holy Trinity – also known as the Godhead.

Before proceeding any further, let us first establish the definition of signs. According to Oxford dictionary, here are some definitions of 'sign' that we can evaluate:

- A notice on public display that gives information or instructions in a written or symbolic form
- An object, quality, or event whose presence or occurrence indicates the probable presence or occurrence of something else
- Authorize by attaching a signature
- Write (one's name) for purposes of identification or authorization
- Write one's name on (a letter, card, document, etc.) to identify oneself as the writer or sender
- Something regarded as an indication of what is happening or going to happen
- A gesture or action used to convey information or an instruction

In the book of Psalms 8:3, the scriptures narrate the following: *When I consider Your heavens, the work of Your fingers, The moon and the stars, which You have ordained.*

This peculiar verse of scripture concedes that the moon and stars are not merely works of God's hand, but instead, the works of his fingers. But are these the same fingers that first wrote the Ten Commandments on the tables of stone given to Moses or are they not? (Exodus 31:18). And what does it actually mean when the scriptures state that the heavens declare God's glory? Are the sun, moon and stars signatures of the Biblical God? Did the Biblical God create the solar system and our universe?

We shall never know, some have said. We shall never know, some will say, because we were not there. 'We shall never know,' so 'they' say, but who are they?

1. The Sun is a celestial symbol of the Father

2. The Moon is an extra-terrestrial symbol of the Son

3. The Stars are the celestial symbol of the Holy Ghost

Considering this is volume 2, let's start with number 2 - the symbol of 'Jesus'. The same Jesus Albert Einstein perceived, felt and almost knew.

"As a child I received instruction both in the Bible and in the Talmud. I am a Jew, but I am enthralled by the luminous figure of the Nazarene... No one can read the Gospels without feeling the actual presence of Jesus. His personality pulsates in every word. No myth is filled with such life."

- Albert Einstein

THE

MOON

'And He [Jesus] was transfigured before them. His face shone like the sun, and His clothes became as white as light.'

- Matthew 17:2

- After previous visits to the moon in search of water, an Indian lunar exploration team recently confirmed that a substantial amount of water is present on the moon. The water found on the moon was confirmed by the National Aeronautics and Space Administration (NASA). In 2009, a satellite slammed into a crater (a hollowed dent) on the moon and about 24 gallons of water filled the hole from the impact. Subsequently, on November 13 2009, scientists from NASA's Lunar Crater Observation and Sensing Satellite announced unequivocally that there is water on the moon and plenty of it. It is now believed that water on the moon is naturally forming and can perpetually exist through man's intervention. This startling discovery has been an exciting yet strange one for astronomers to fully grasp because the moon is lifeless and does not have an atmosphere like our planet earth to contain and preserve water. Naturally, any exposed ice or water on the moon would be quickly vaporised by sunlight and lost to space, so the only possible place for water or ice to exist on the moon would be in its shadowed craters, which often result from the ancient meteorites and micrometeorites' crashes on the moon's surface.

This recent discovery of water on the lifeless moon acutely illuminates the biblical narrative of the water found in the lifeless body of Jesus, as recorded in John 19:28–35. Jesus, when close to his death, had been bleeding profusely from his inflicted wounds. His body was covered in blood when he asked for a drink of water. He was thirsty but was given a sponge soaked in vinegar. A few moments after this, he died. Then one of the Roman soldiers, in an attempt to verify his death, pierced the side of Jesus' wounded body with a spear, and instead of finding a flowing blood stream, water also came out of his body. (Notice that the water found on the moon was discovered in the same manner that water was found in the lifeless body of Christ – somebody crashed into the side of the **cratered** moon just like the Roman solder pierced the **wounded** side of the body of Jesus.)

So why and how is it that the dehydrated, lifeless body of Jesus could stream out water? Jesus highlighted this mystery for us in the story of the Samaritan woman whom he met at the well of Jacob in John 4:7–10. Here as well, Jesus was thirsty and he asked for a drink of water from the Samaritan woman, but she refused to give him water because he was a Jew and she was a Samaritan and it was not customary for both cultures to mingle in those days. Jesus said to the Samaritan woman: *'If you knew the gift of God, and who it is who says to you, 'Give Me a drink,' you would have asked Him, and He would have given you living water.'* (John 4:10)

- There is only one moon that orbits the rotating earth, so all people over the continents of the world who see the moon see the same moon, and this is unique, considering other planets in our solar system have several moons or no moon

24

at all. Planet earth has only one moon!! And this moon is the only mediator between the sun and the earth.1st Timothy 2:5–6 amplify the above statement allegorically: *'For there is one God and one Mediator between God and men, the Man Christ Jesus, who gave Himself a ransom for all, to be testified in due time.'*

- According to forensic astronomy, the earth's moon is the child of the earth. It is said that at the forming stage of the budding earth, a body of rock and mass came from a distance and collided with the earth, hitting it at an oblique angle and, consequently, dashing through the forming earth, took from it a yarn of rock pieces, dust and ice that bonded together through a heating process and created our present moon that orbits around the earth. In addition, astronomers have confirmed that the moon's birth is **unmistakably miraculous**: a more direct blow at the forming earth could have utterly obliterated its formation process and the angle at which the forming earth was hit made it possible to have an adequate sizeable moon that can stabilise the earth.

This story of the moon's formation is a much-talked-about scientific phenomenon, just like the birth of Jesus Christ. Time and again in the Bible, Jesus refers to himself as 'the son of man'. The earth, in Hebrew, is 'Adamah', from which Adam (meaning earth and man) was shaped and carved. When we compare Jesus' description of himself as the son of man with the description of the moon as the child of the earth, it is interesting to find that both narratives intricately synchronise.

Further, we have also learned from the scriptures that the birth of Jesus was not in the natural way in which every man or woman came into this world, but that Jesus was born to the Virgin Mary. Here are a few scriptures to confirm the **miraculous birth of Jesus** and scriptures to show his description as the son of man: Luke 1:27–35, Matthew 9:6.

In light of the above narrative from forensic astronomy and its scriptural correspondence, note that the size and mass of the moon is smaller in comparison to the size and mass of the earth, just as Jesus often described himself in the scriptures as one smaller to man. He never referred to himself as a fully grown man, but always as a son of man even when he spoke of ascending to and descending from heaven (John 3:13). Also note in passing, that the forensic narrative of the moon's birth mainly illustrates the representation of the birth of Jesus as the son of man.

- The gravitational pull of the moon (as well as the sun) around the rotating earth is known to cause the waves and tides of waters in the ocean. Scientists have confirmed that it is the moon that creates the moving sound of waters in the ocean. However, it is not merely a one-off sound that results from the gravitational pull of the moon but a continuing rhythmical sound! This is important to note because the apostle John, when visited by Jesus (in his celestial body and sun-like countenance – Revelation 1:15b), described his voice as the sound of many waters; that is to say, Jesus spoke to him with the voice of many waters – a rhythmical sound (Selah: meaning pause and think). In addition, it has been said by some astronomers that when a full moon appears it tends to awaken the life force on earth and can cause all sort of excessive emotional excitement because of its pulling effect. The stars and the sun in their full brilliance of strength do the exact opposite; they can turn a forest into a desert. What is also interesting about this description of the moon's pulling effect is that when Jesus spoke of himself in John 12:32, he said the following: *'And I, if I am lifted up from the earth, will draw all people to Myself.'*

- There is a fascinating scripture in the Bible that certain

27

students of astronomy like to mock and ridicule. Revelation 6:12 – *'I looked when He opened the sixth seal, and behold, there was a great earthquake; and the sun became black as sackcloth of hair,* **and the moon became like blood.***'* The same scripture is narrated in the book of Acts 2:19–20 as the following: *'I* [God speaking] *will show wonders in heaven above and* **signs in the earth beneath: blood** *and fire and vapour of smoke. The sun shall be turned into darkness,* **and the moon into blood,** *before the coming of the great and awesome day of the Lord.'*

Certain Bible critics who are acquainted with the studies of astronomy make a mockery of 'the moon turning to blood'. They express that the writers of the scriptures had primitive knowledge of astronomy and as such exaggerated the rare phenomenon of the blood-red moon as having spiritual significance of any sort. They also express that the rare event of the blood-red moon had been reoccurring before the Torah was written, so how could it have any significant relation to the lordship of Jesus? But what they fail to understand is that the moon turning blood red is a representation of Jesus on the cross shedding his 'red blood' for humanity. The Apostle John expressed in the book of Revelation 13:8 that the death of Jesus transpired from the foundation and creation of the world. An odd statement but spiritually incisive and profound! God's past is man's future ('pause and think'). What causes the blood-red moon is a symbolic mystery that lies within the earth's shadow.

Invariably, the earth's atmosphere diffuses the light it receives from the sun, showering and providing warm rays of light from the sun to our plants for photosynthesis and energising our planet and surroundings with solar energy. But much like the human body, the earth also discharges its harmful rays of light through its atmosphere. Similar to the harmful sun rays that are filtered through the earth's atmosphere, polluted air and gases (from human lungs and motor vehicles), ashes and dusts (from volcanic eruptions) sometimes gather in the air to discharge red light rays through the earth's atmosphere.

When this process of atmospheric excretion is in transit, the colour lights of blue and green in the atmosphere of the earth are dispersed and scattered by the polluted atmospheric gases, permitting only the red light to travel straight through the earth's exterior atmosphere. Consequently, the edges of the earth and the outline of its shadow are lit with a red glow of light! During a lunar eclipse – when the sun, earth, and moon are evenly aligned, or very closely so, with the earth in the middle – the moon passes behind the shadow of the earth, and as it's no longer being illuminated by the sun, it reflects the filtered red glow from the earth's shadow. The polluted gases and the filtered red rays passing through the earth's atmosphere are responsible for colouring the moon red.

However, sometimes the moon 'may appear' red in the sky if the earth's atmosphere that's facing the moon is saturated with polluted reddish-looking gases and dust particles, in which case we are viewing the moon through the clouded lens of the earth's discoloured reddish atmosphere. But the moon also 'turns' red if it is reflecting the red glow residing within the earth's shadow as its moonlight! In which case, the sun is hidden and blocked by the earth from the moon's view, and this can only transpire during a lunar eclipse. The scripture's narration of the 'moon turning red' is obviously the latter, and not the former.

The astronomical narrative of the blood-red moon precisely illuminates the biblical narrative of Jesus' crucifixion and death. The scriptures narrate that 'we' crucified Jesus, though not merely with our hands and feet. It was for our sins that he streamed with blood as he was whipped, flogged and crucified on the cross. It is our secret and public sins, dirt, evil motives and deeds that nailed him to the cross, just like the polluted gases and dusts from the earth directing the red light to the moon. Jesus' shed blood was for humanity's redemption, and reconciliation with a Holy God who cannot tolerate sin, yet love sinners (this Biblical oxymoron is intricately illuminated in my book – The Mystery).

Like the harmful rays of the sun filtered out of the earth by the earth's atmosphere, the red glow light outside the body of the earth, channelled by polluted dusts and gases in the earth, reflected by the moon (during a lunar eclipse), is symbolic of Jesus' shed blood and death commemorating the Father's judgement of humanity's sins. John 5:22–23 reveals: *'For the Father judges no one, but has committed all judgment to the Son, that all should honor the Son just as they honor the Father. He who does not honor the Son does not honor the Father who sent Him.'*

According to the Bible, we have all been born with the nature of sin (Psalms 51:5-6) since the day that Adam and Eve fell, and it is for this reason that Jesus gave his sinless life as the sacrificial lamb for the atonement of our sins. Some Biblical teachers have even speculated that Jesus died of a broken heart as we find in the book of Psalms 69:20–21. He was rejected by men (still is), and also alienated from the immortality and divinity of his Father at the cross as he took our sinful place. Though he had no kinship blood of the first man - Adam, in him because of his unnatural and miraculous birth through the Virgin Mary, yet he suffered both physical AND spiritual death, just like Adam, and his descendants – which we are. The blood-red moon is a constant reminder of Jesus' sacrifice and death for humanity. It is a sign of his shed blood.

Furthermore, as the scripture avows in Acts 2:19–20, there is an imminent astronomic wonder to be anticipated before the return of the Lord Jesus to earth, but astronomers struggle to understand what this wonder could possibly be:

'I [God speaking] *will show wonders in heaven above and signs in the earth beneath:* **blood** *and* **fire** *and* **vapour of smoke.** **The sun shall be turned into darkness, and the moon into blood, before the coming of the great and awesome day of the Lord.'**

'The sun turning into darkness' is a solar eclipse, and 'the moon becoming blood red', (or not reflecting sunlight) is a lunar eclipse.

As previously illustrated, a lunar eclipse is when the sun, earth and moon are evenly aligned, or very closely so, with the earth in the middle − which blocks the sun from the moon and the moon from the sun, thereby preventing the sun from illuminating the moon, and positioning the earth to cast its shadow or unwanted (red) light from the sun on the surface of the moon. A solar eclipse is when the sun, moon and earth are evenly aligned, or very closely so, with the moon in the middle − which blocks the sun from the earth and the earth from the sun, thereby obstructing immediate sunlight from the earth during day.

Now here is the astronomical wonder: If the sun becoming dark (from our view on earth) is a solar eclipse and the moon turning red is a lunar eclipse, and the scriptures have revealed that these events will transpire before the notable day of the Lord's coming, then this means that a solar eclipse and a lunar eclipse will co-exist and occur simultaneously prior to the coming of Jesus. 'But how can this be?' you may ask, because the moon is closest to the sun in the event of a solar eclipse and the earth is closest to the sun in the event of a lunar eclipse.

Certainly, this will be a spectacular sight to see as it has never been seen before! This astronomical wonder will transpire for the sole purpose of glorifying Jesus as the son of man (represented by the moon).

During a lunar eclipse, when the earth is positioned between the sun and moon and moon and sun, if the edges and shadow of the earth contain a filtered red glow light that's channelled by the polluted dust particles from the earth, then the earth's shadow 'on its own' can reflect this red light to the moon (without the aid of sunlight from the sun to earth). It is at this time that the Father God will exterminate the fire of the sun and all other star lights in the heavens, and the extermination of these billions of stars 'or '**celestial fires**' will cause the emission and spread of '**vapours and clouds of smoke**' in the cosmos and the earth's atmosphere.

At this precise moment, all creation everywhere will only see the apparent glow of the blood red-moon (reflected from the earth's shadow), in awe and enchantment, as all other star lights will be turned off!! This is the sign that will signify the return of the Lord Jesus!

In Matthew 24:29–30, Jesus narrates: *'Immediately after the tribulation of those days the sun will be darkened, and the moon will not give its light* [from the sun]*; the stars will fall from heaven, and the powers of the heavens will be shaken. Then **the sign** of the Son of Man* [the red moon] *will appear in heaven, and then all the tribes of the earth will mourn, and they will see the*

Son of Man coming on the clouds of heaven with power and great glory.'

Revelations 1:7 adds: *'Behold, He is coming with clouds, and every eye will see Him,* **even they who pierced Him** [symbolic of the blood shed of Jesus]. *And all the tribes of the earth will mourn because of Him. Even so, Amen.'* (Also, see Acts 1:11 and Zechariah 12:10 for more references)

The blood-red moon 'alone' in the sky is the macrographic representation and sign that will precede the appearance of the Lord Jesus on his second arrival to earth. Today, the blood-red moon symbolises the crucifixion and shed blood of Jesus for humanity's redemption, but one day, the scriptures promise that the rare blood-red moon will be the last view from this world as we know it.

- The moon is both terrestrial and celestial. Astronomers cannot travel to the stars or our sun for a friendly visit, because these celestial lights have zero tolerance for the terrestrial. However, like the moon, Jesus not only refers to himself as a son of man but also as the son of God. All through scriptures it is evident that Jesus maintained a dual identity (John 9:35–37 and John 3:13).

In reference to Abraham who God visited in times past, God said in Genesis 13:16: *'And **I will make your seed as the***

dust of the earth; *so that if a man could number the dust of the earth, then your seed also could be numbered.'* Also, in Genesis 15:5: *'Then He brought him outside and said,* **"Look now toward heaven, and count the stars** *if you are able to number them."* *And He said to him,* **"So shall your seed be."** God compared the seed of Abraham to the dust of the earth and the stars in heaven. The scriptures later reveal to us that the seed promised to Abraham was inherent in Isaac and Jacob but had not yet been realised. As shown in Genesis 28:13–14, Jacob's encounter with God revealed that the promised seed was a continuing promise:

'And behold, the Lord stood above it and said: "I am the Lord God of Abraham your father and the God of Isaac; the land on which you lie I will give to you and your descendants. **Also your seed shall be as the dust of the earth**; *you shall spread abroad to the west and the east, to the north and the south;* **and in you** [i.e. the loins of Abraham, Isaac and Jacob, symbolising the old covenant] **and in your seed** [which is 'Christ Jesus', symbolising the new covenant] *all the families of the earth shall be blessed.*

To David, who also came from the loins of Abraham (Matthew 1:1), God reiterated the promised seed of Abraham in Jeremiah 33:22: *'**As the host of heaven cannot be**

36

numbered, nor the sand of the sea measured, so will I multiply the seed of David My servant...' The apostle Paul in the New Testament later confirmed that this seed was Christ Jesus. Galatians 3:16: *'Now to Abraham and his Seed were the promises made.* **He does not say, "And to seeds," as of many, but as of one, "And to your Seed," who is Christ.'**

The moon, which is an extraterrestrial symbol of Jesus Christ, is both terrestrial like the dust of the earth and celestial like the stars of the heavens. Additionally, Jesus' miraculous birth through the Virgin Mary showed that he was *the seed of the woman* that was recorded in Genesis 3:15. Naturally, every human birth requires the seed of a man and the womb of a woman. However, the life of Jesus on earth was different in that he was conceived in a woman without the seed of a man; and as such he led two separate lives simultaneously! His life as a human being from the womb of a woman symbolised the terrestrial and his inherent divinity by his unnatural and miraculous birth symbolised the celestial, just like the moon's dual realities.

- In the book of John 14:7–11, Jesus said the following to his disciples: *'If you had known Me, you would have known My Father also; and from now on you know Him and have seen Him. Philip said to Him, Lord, show us the Father, and it is sufficient for us. Jesus said to him, Have I been with you so long, and yet you have not known Me, Philip? He who has seen Me has seen the Father; so how can you say, 'Show us the Father'? Do you not believe that I am in the Father, and the Father in Me? The words that I speak to you I do not speak on My own authority; but the Father who dwells in Me does the works. Believe Me that I am in the Father and the Father in Me, or else believe Me for the sake of the works themselves.'*

I can empathise with Philip's reasoning here when he asked Jesus to show them the Father, and I'm not sure that Jesus' reply at the time sufficed, despite his explanation. The spirit of revelation had not yet come to reveal the mystery about Jesus' identity with divinity (John 16:12-13).

According to Jesus, he said that if any man had seen him, then that man had seen the Father as well.

Jesus also said that he was in the Father and the Father was in him, which proved difficult at the time to fully comprehend.

However, if we carefully examine the relationship between the moon and the sun, it symbolically represents what Jesus was trying to explain to his disciples. The sun is primarily full of hydrogen and helium and the light that comes from the sun is reflected by the moon to the earth. The light we see from the moon does not at all belong to the moon; it's actually from the sun and belongs to the sun. The moon, as well as reflecting light from the sun to the earth, provides warmth to the earth so that the earth receives both light and heat from the sun even at night, just like it is during the day. This shows what Jesus meant when he was speaking to Philip and the other disciples, explaining to them that those who had seen him had also seen the Father, just as he who sees the moon is also looking at the sun. After all, it is the sun that lights up the moon, and without the sun, we cannot see the moon. For the Father to be in the Son, the Son has to be void of his own will and wants, living in total dependence on the Father. Jesus, again (in John 5:30a) described himself in like manner: *'I can of Myself do nothing. As I hear, I judge; and My judgment is righteous, because I do not seek My own will but the will of the Father who sent Me.'*

The moon has very little gravity in comparison to earth; it has no clouds to sustain an atmosphere, and though it is the closest body of mass to the earth, it is drier than any desert on earth. Its interior does not actually contain the astrophysical contents of hydrogen and helium in the sun; yet it is the direct supplier of the sun's heat and light to the earth. In comparison, Jesus' earthly body scarcely reflected a celestial light while living on earth, so he said to his disciples, if it's hard for you to believe that the Father is 'visibly' in me, just as the sunlight is not 'visibly' in the moon but on its surface, *'believe Me for the sake of the works themselves'*; that is to say, the function of the moon is the same as the function of the sun to the earth.

Time and again, astronomers have confirmed the uniqueness of our moon in that it is the only eligible body of mass in our solar system that can carry out similar activities like the sun to our planet while simultaneously protecting and stabilising the weather seasons on earth. Jesus is also represented by a star, which is why Jesus could say to the disciples that the Father (represented by the sun) is 'visibly and tangibly' in him. After Jesus' resurrection, Jesus as 'Christ' is represented by a star and the star is the symbol of his heavenly association with divinity while the moon, pointing to his life before death, is a symbol of his earthly association with divinity. Further, it is from the body of the moon that we can better view and examine sunlight than to directly examine the light of the sun from the sun itself! The body of the sun is outworn and outshone by its exterior light. Just like Jesus said to Philip in John 14:9 – *'He who has seen Me has seen the Father; so how can you say, 'Show us the*

Father'? In other words, we cannot handle seeing the Father physically without altering our physical state of matter.

- As frequently practised, astronomers use an optical laser light to observe and measure the motion and activities of the distant moon from planet earth. This laser light pointed at the distant moon has been said to have quadrillions of photons with the hope that a few grains bounce back to the earth. The optical device has helped to measure with precision as little as one millimetre in the motion of the distant moon. In light of the above, it is evident that the best practice of astronomers is to use an instrument of light to measure a body of light!

Jesus said in John 5:39 *'Search the Scriptures; for in them ye think ye have eternal life, and they are they which testify of me.'* In other words, the written word of scriptures helps to examine the living word of scriptures, and both are identities of the same Jesus! As recorded in John 1:1–14 and Genesis 1:2–3, Jesus is the incarnated word from the beginning that was present with the Holy Spirit and the Father, who later manifested in human flesh. In Psalm 119:105, King David describes the word of God as *'a lamp to his feet and a light to his path'*. Psalm 36:9b sums it all up:

'In Your light we see light' – just like the optical laser light used to examine the lunar moon, and the written word of scriptures' correlation with the manifested word in human form, the scriptures, alternatively known as 'The Word of God', are representative of Jesus. The Father and the Holy Spirit are not 'The Incarnated Word' but the voice and power behind it. Revelation 19:13 further reveals the name of Jesus as 'The Word of God' - *'He was clothed with a robe dipped in blood, and His name is called The Word of God.'*

- The moon is known to stare directly at planet earth while orbiting the rotating earth and its union with our planet appears to be tightly bound. Because of this, the moon and earth has been labelled a 'couple' by several astronomers. Similarly, the scripture identifies Jesus as a bridegroom who will come for his bride on earth – the Church. In John 3:29, John the Baptist said of Jesus: 'He who has the bride is the bridegroom; but the friend of the bridegroom, who stands and hears him, rejoices greatly because of the bridegroom's voice. Therefore this joy of mine is fulfilled.' Ephesians 5:25 adds: *'Husbands, love your wives, just as Christ also loved the church and gave Himself for her.'*

- In times past, there have been discrepancies about the

moon's rotational behaviour around the earth. If we look at the moon on different nights, we will find that it appears to show the same feature. This observation led some to think the moon did not rotate. Some astronomers proposed that one side of the moon was heavier than the other and is pulled by gravity to always face the earth, which is why it exhibits the same side. But it was later realised that the moon rotates at the same speed as it orbits the rotating earth, which is why we continue to see the same face of the moon over and over again. Hebrews 13:8 describes Jesus in like manner: *'Jesus Christ is the same yesterday, today and forever.'*

- The book of Psalms 84:11 states: *'For the lord God is a sun and shield: the lord will give grace and glory: no good thing will he withhold from them that walk uprightly.'* This verse of scripture carries a poignant insight. In Matthew 22:43–45, Jesus (also known as the son of David) esteemed the prophetic insight that David showed in his knowledge and understanding of the Godhead: *'He [Jesus] said to them [the Pharisees], "How then does David in the Spirit call Him 'Lord,' saying: 'The Lord said to my Lord "Sit at My right hand, till I make Your enemies Your footstool"'? If David then calls Him 'Lord,' how is He his Son?" And no one was able to answer Him a word…'*

43

Evidently, David recognised the difference in the lordship of the Father and the Son and expressed yet another prophetic insight on this subject in Psalm 84:11 - *For the lord God is a sun and shield: the lord will give grace and glory...*

Glory in the scriptures is often associated with the sun and is also a representation for the Father (John 17:5), while grace is affiliated with salvation through Jesus (Ephesians 2:7-8). The moon's protecting gravity around the rotating earth has always been a shield to planet earth. Without the moon's close proximity to planet earth, the earth's vulnerability to the gravitational pull of larger planets like Jupiter would have caused the earth to tilt and topple over.

If this happens, unpredictable weather seasons and a global flooding will ensue, thereby causing our planet to become inhabitable. Because of the significant contribution of our moon to life on earth, astronomers often describe the moon as the stabiliser and protector of our planet. Synchronically, the moon bears a unique resemblance to the saving grace of Jesus for humanity, as recorded in the Bible.

Also, in times past, planet earth has suffered asteroids and meteorite attacks. However, the moon has suffered greater impacts from meteorites and asteroids attacks. Many have questioned why it is that more craters (i.e. wounds) are found on the moon's surface than the planet earth. Astronomers speculate several reasons for this: 1) there is no meteorological, biological or geological activity on the moon to help eliminate the craters 2) the moon does not have an atmosphere like our planet, which makes it more vulnerable to suffer greater meteor impacts than earth. 3) It is also a postulate of reason among space astronomers that the moon acts as a shield to protect the earth from meteorites heading towards it. Profoundly, the scriptures also provide a lucid reason for this enigma - the moon, which is a shield to our planet, was purposed by God to be a reminder of the sufferings that Jesus bore for humanity on the cross. At the cross, Jesus identified with the sufferings of humanity and even now, he identifies with the sufferings of his persecuted church. Before Saul's transformation to "Apostle Paul", Jesus appeared to him as he embarked on another journey to slaughter more of his disciples. Acts 9:4–5 narrates: *'Then he [Saul] fell to the ground, and heard a voice saying to him, "Saul, Saul, why are you persecuting Me?" And he said, "Who are You, Lord?" Then the Lord said, "I am Jesus, whom you are persecuting. It is hard for you to kick against the goads."*

In Philippians 3:10, the apostle Paul later wrote of his relationship with Jesus: *'That I may know Him and the power of His resurrection, and* **the fellowship of His sufferings,** *being conformed to His death.'*

Romans 15:3 adds: *For even Christ [Jesus] did not please Himself; but as it is written, "The reproaches of those who reproached You fell on Me."*

- In John 8:12 and Matthew 5:14, Jesus expressed that he is the light of the world and also describes his followers in like manner. John 12:46 confirms: *'I have come as a light into the world, that whoever believes in Me should not abide in darkness.'* Metaphorically, what Jesus is saying here is that he is a light in darkness, which fitly describes the primary function of the moon. John 8:12 also informs: *Then Jesus spoke to them again, saying, "I am the light of the world. He who follows Me shall not walk in darkness, but have the light of life."* It is interesting to find that Jesus continues to describe the world as the night every time he makes reference to himself as the light. Another example of this can be found in John 11:9–10: *'Jesus answered, "Are there not twelve hours in the day?* [Notice Jesus' clever remark by quickly dividing the hours of the day from night in this first line.] *If anyone walks in the day, he does not stumble, because he sees the light of this world. But if one walks in the night, he stumbles, because the light is not in him.'*

46

In this text of scripture, Jesus as the 'son of man' refers to the Father in heaven as the giver of light to earth (like the sun at noon). However, in verse ten, he refers to himself as the preceding light from the Father that seeks to dwell in the hearts of men who walks in darkness – like the moon at night. The symbolic meaning of this text is the reason followers of Jesus often express that they have him in their hearts. To accept Jesus in one's heart is exposited in the scriptures as making peace with God and reconciling with the divine.

Furthermore, Jesus also expressed that his followers are sent to the world as he is sent from the Father (John 17:18). Similarly, moonlight is a light sent from the sun to the earth.

- In recent years, astronomers have discovered that the moon continues to retreat from our planet earth at an annual measure of three inches ('3'- Selah). They fear that if the moon continues to retreat from the earth, the earth will die without the moon's constancy. The moon's function in assisting earth with stability of seasons and moderate ocean heights can be lost if this continues. However, astronomers have realised that the friction from the waterbeds of the earth is what pushes the moon forward and that the earth is in fact responsible for the retreat of the moon.

In addition, astronomers have observed that the moon's perpetual retreat is combined with an accelerating speed! They do not understand why. They are perplexed as this observation raises more questions than answers. The scriptures state that in the last days of our planet's existence, many will drift away from believing in the gospel of Jesus. Additionally, the scriptures state that the love and warmth in the hearts of men and women will grow cold, and that many will exalt the knowledge of 'self' against the knowledge of God by seeking to eliminate divinity and deify humanity (2 Timothy 3:1–5 and 2 Timothy 4:3). The earth pushing the moon away is symbolic of humans pushing the gospel of Jesus away, and the speed that the moon ferociously continues to gather is the sign that the second coming of Jesus is drawing nearer!

THE NEW MOON

(Moon + Sun = New Moon)

In the Chinese calendar, the beginning of the month is marked by the dark moon, also known as the astronomical new moon. The new moon in its original meaning of first crescent marks the beginning of the month in lunar calendars like Islam, and in lunisolar calendars (e.g. Hebrew, Hindu and Buddhist). Most predominant religions and traditions recognise and uphold the significance of the new moon. Even Hollywood teen wolves and vampires want a piece of the new moon. But what is the meaning of the new moon according to the Bible?

What does it represent? According to Colossians 2:16–17, the new moon is a symbolic meaning for Christ Jesus: '*So let no one judge you in food or in drink, or regarding a festival or a new moon or sabbaths, which are a shadow of things to come, but the substance* [of it all] *is of Christ.'*

Evidently, this verse of scripture implicitly states that the new moon is a fore shadow of Christ Jesus. In John 16:16–21, Jesus allegorically defines the new moon as 'his journey' to and from the Father. But before we go there, let us consider the definition of the new moon in astronomy.

The new moon is the lunar phase that occurs when the moon, in its monthly orbital motion around the earth lies between the earth and the sun, and is in conjunction with the sun as seen from planet earth. At this time, it is the dark and unilluminated portion of the moon that faces almost directly toward earth. Consequently, the moon is not at all visible or partly visible to the naked eyes on earth at night.

Please also note that a solar eclipse may sometimes coincide with the new moon and as previously highlighted - a solar eclipse is when the sun, moon, and earth are evenly aligned, or very closely so, with the moon in the middle, so that the sun cannot view the earth and the earth cannot view the sun. Solar eclipses (especially a total solar eclipse) can be very frightening to people who are unaware of their astronomical explanation. When it occurs, the sun may seem to disappear during day because the sun is covered and hidden by the moon from earth. Consequently, the earth's sky can become dark in a matter of minutes.

During the crucifixion of Jesus, before he died, this is exactly what happened - a sudden night fell shortly after noon! The book of Matthew 27:45 and Mark 15:33 records that a sudden darkness came over the whole land of Israel from the *'sixth to the ninth hour'* prior to Jesus' death (which is equivalent to 12:00pm – 3:00pm GMT). Luke 23:45 narrates: *Then the sun was darkened* [meaning a solar eclipse occurred]*, and the veil of the temple was torn in two* [suggesting a new chapter in history had emerged].' Notice that this eclipse lasted for a three-hour period (the scripture's precision is impeccably remarkable as 'three' here again represents the Holy Trinity). Also, Jesus, who was and is the second expression of the trinity, 'incidentally' died at the age of 33. (Selah).

Jesus' crucifixion and death was marked by both a new moon and a solar eclipse. As his divine transition from earth began to escape his human body, the moon (representing Jesus) moved toward the sun (representing the Father). However, Jesus (who was once represented by the extra-terrestrial moon) at the time of his crucifixion had become like the dark terrestrial earth – away from the illuminated union of the moon and sun, much like the intimacy between a son and father, Jesus was obstructed from his fellowship with his Father at the cross because he bore the sins of humanity. His association with the fallen Adam (i.e. humanity) in the peril of death at the cross is the reason he cried out *'My God, my God, why have you forsaken me?'* Taking our sinful place through the penalty of sin, by his death - according to Romans 6:23, Jesus for the first time prayed like mortal men and addressed his Father foreignly, calling him 'God'. But before he took his last breath, he returned again to himself and declared in faith: *'... "Father" in your hands I commit my spirit.'*

His transition away from his extra-terrestrial position as the moon (i.e. his divine connection with the Father) was only temporary because his death at the cross (symbolic of his union with the abyss of the earth) was for the sole purpose of resurrection and newness of life - just as the moon's closer alignment and conjunction with the sun ultimately engenders a new moon.

N
W ┼ E
S

Invariably, at the cross, Jesus died for the world. But much like the darkness of the earth that ensued from the occurrence of the solar eclipse - caused by the moon's initial transit from its natural ordained boundary (symbolic of Jesus death), Jesus would later return to the previous life he lived but with a greater power. This was his resurrection! The new moon phenomenon compasses the departure and return of the moon to its ordained boundary - similar to the death and resurrection of Christ Jesus in his physical form. The moon alone cannot adequately explain the resurrection phenomena, only a new moon or the birth of a star may suffice! (We shall find more evidences for Jesus' resurrection in the astronomic narrative of the stars.)

Though a solar eclipse is responsible for the darkness of the earth, the new moon occurrence portrays a dark view of the moon to the earth. This astronomic information symbolically shows that Jesus experienced both physical (solar eclipse) and spiritual (new moon) death. As revealed in the narratives of the scriptures, Jesus suffered rejection from both humanity and his Father at the cross (Isaiah 53:1-5)! But the Father later restored life to Jesus through his resurrection; just like the return of the renewed moon, which we call 'the new moon'.

Please also note the following insight in relation to Jesus' death at the cross - for Jesus to physically die, he had to be separated from his divine relationship with the Father at the cross. This is why he first cried out: *'My God, my God, why have you forsaken me?'* before confessing: *'It is finished'* (John 19:30). Jesus could not easily die as one who was divinely incarnated but could only die as a mortal. The separation from the Father was necessary; otherwise he would not have physically died. His eternal existence, while living in a human form on earth, was embedded in his union with the Father. The divine nature of his life as 'the Son in the Father' and 'the Father in the Son' is the reason Jesus was capable of enduring more violent sufferings than any human possibly could. Not even the Biblical Samson could withstand what Jesus had to endure on the way to his crucifixion at the cross. His separation from the Father was his first death, which is spiritual in nature and represented by the new moon phenomenon. The new moon then brought sudden darkness to earth – described as a solar eclipse in astronomy, and this solar eclipse at Jesus' crucifixion represented Jesus' physical death. The revelation of Jesus' spiritual and physical death is just like our biblical origin story at the Garden of Eden (Genesis 2:17). After Adam and Eve's disobedience of God's law by eating the forbidden fruit, they first died spiritually and it seemed like nothing as dire as death had transpired. But it was their spiritual death – their 'separation from the Father' – that later ensued in a physical death.

In retrospect, and for our ongoing emphasis, a new moon is

when the moon aligns itself with the sun, which consequently results in the appearance of a dark silhouette moon or a crescent moon. Finally, here is what Jesus had to say about himself as relating to the new moon in the book of John 16:16–21: *'A little while, and **you will not see Me; and again a little while, and you will see Me, because I go to the Father."** Then some of His disciples said among themselves, **"What is this that He says to us, 'A little while, and you will not see Me; and again a little while, and you will see Me'; and, 'because I go to the Father'?"** They said therefore, **"What is this that He says, 'A little while'?** We do not know what He is saying." Now Jesus knew that they desired to ask Him, and He said to them, **"Are you inquiring among yourselves about what I said, 'A little while, and you will not see Me; and again a little while, and you will see Me'?** Most assuredly, I say to you that you will weep and lament, but the world will rejoice; and you will be sorrowful, but your sorrow will be turned into joy. A woman, when she is in labor, has sorrow because her hour has come; but as soon as she has given birth to the child, she no longer remembers the anguish, for joy that a human being has been born into the world.'*

In verse 25, Jesus continued speaking: *'These things I have spoken to you in proverbs: but the time is coming, when I will no longer speak to you in proverbs, but I will show you plainly of the Father.'*

Evidently, in John 16:16–21 Jesus described his absence from the earth. He categorically explained that the world (loving and living in darkness - John 3:19–20) will celebrate his temporary absence from the earth, but his followers (loving and living in his light - John 3:21) will be sad when he is absent. However, he also compares his temporary absence from the earth to the reproductive process of giving birth to a child because his absence from earth will ultimately result in a closer presence with his Father. Therefore, his return from the Father will be anew, like the delivery of a newborn child – like the 'new moon'!

Furthermore, as the sun's distance from the earth is about 400 times the moon's distance, and the sun's diameter is about 400 times the moon's diameter, these coordinating ratios - approximately the same - ensure that the sun and moon as seen from the earth appear as the same size. This astronomic insight evokes yet another deeply profound mystery, showing humanity that, indeed, Jesus is the epitome of the Father sent to earth to reconcile humanity to the Father.

As recorded in the Bible, Jesus did not merely point the way to the Father, but also claimed that 'he is the way' to the Father. In John 10:30 he said: 'I and my Father are one'; and in the book of John 14:6, he said: '... I am the way, the truth, and the life: no man comes to the Father, but by me.' This latter verse of scripture is perhaps the most controversial and fascinating scripture as viewed in today's society. Its astronomical meaning is just as fascinating when we examine the paradigm relationship between the sun and moon from the perspectives of NASA's space voyages and human efforts to travel into space.

According to Hugh Wilson, in an MSN article published in December 2011, the fastest spacecraft yet devised by humans took 'three' days to get an astronaut to the moon, and our very best technology would take nine months to get an astronaut to Mars.

As previously illustrated, the moon (representing Jesus), like the sun (representing the Father), sustains life on earth. It provides earth with light, heat, gravity and balance. Also, the moon is the 'only absolute' ground and path man has 'physically' stood and walked on in outer space. It is also the closest man has been to the sun in space travel and the furthest ground away from earth that humans have physically travelled to! Other space travels in the celestial sphere are conducted by NASA's explorer machineries or robotic probes, similar to window shopping or looking through the windows of a house to view its contents; these space explorer voyage findings are not as authentic and inerrant as man's physical visit to the moon.

The moon is like 'the door' (and not windows) to outer space, just like Jesus' description of himself in John 10:7–9.

To closely view the sun in its celestial sphere, there has only been one place for humans to visit beside the terrestrial and ordinary earth, and that is the moon.

Just like the words of Jesus in the gospel of John – no man comes to the Father but by the Son.

Charlie's walk on the moon

'The documentary **'In the Shadow of the Moon'** *includes the story of Charlie Duke, one of the Apollo 16 astronauts launched to the moon in 1972. While the command ship orbited the moon, Duke and another astronaut landed the lunar module Orion on the moon's surface. After three days of running experiments and collecting lunar rocks, the Apollo 16 crew safely returned to earth. Later, Charlie had a spiritual transformation. He said it began when his friend invited him to a Bible study. After the meeting, Charlie prayed to Christ, 'I give you my life, and if you're real come into my life.' He then experienced an indescribable peace. It was so profound that he began to share his story with others. Charlie told them: My walk on the moon lasted three days and it was a great adventure, but my walk with God lasts forever.'*

~ Our Daily Bread (January 31st 2012)

THE SUN

'And God [first] said, let there be light: and there was light.'

– Genesis 1:3

- According to many astronomers, our sun is an ordinary star. It is often called a yellow dwarf because it is smaller in comparison with other stars. However, it is the largest object in the solar system and is located at the heart of our planetary system. Because of its comparison to larger stars, many space astronomers have challenged the sun's superiority and uniqueness over other stars. The primary distinction associated with the sun is its close proximity to our planet, and this is all that should really matter!

In his description of God, Jesus often used an un-extraordinary term. He rarely attributed great titles to God like the prophets of old in the Old Testament. In fact, Jesus never preached about a religion of God, but only spoke of God as his Father. Similarly, our sun has been confirmed by scientists as being the only life-giving star. Its English name, 'sun', derives from the Latin word 'sol', and it is from this Latin name that our planetary system was dubbed 'solar'. The sun is the parent star of our planetary system, which makes our planetary system the only solar system in the universe. Other planetary systems that exist derive their names from their parent stars (parent star is a terminology astronomers use to describe our sun and other planetary system stars.) Our sun doesn't have to be the biggest star in the galaxy. It doesn't even have to seem extraordinary and rare for us to establish its significance above other stars. The sun is planet earth's parent star, just as God is a Father to us. Synchronically, the doctrine and heart of the gospel of Jesus was about our Father.

Furthermore, there are few stars in the cosmos with a size and mass like our sun, known as sun-like stars or proxy stars. And stars with a smaller size and mass like our sun, has been confirmed to live longer than larger stars. This is because larger stars burn so brightly that they exhaust their nuclear fusion energy more quickly. In correlation, small is actually big in the astronomy of stars, and though our sun may seem like other stars, yet every other star in the universe is not the life-giving sun.

- Every star is confirmed by astronomers as belonging to or originating from a cluster of stars. Likewise, astronomers speculate that our sun must have emerged from a star-forming nursery. In the first chapter and verse of Genesis, the reference for God in Hebrew is *Elohim*. However, *Elohim* is plural in meaning and connotes a collective identity of persons as our creator. But as the story of Genesis continues to unfold, a singular identity of the Father is revealed to be the executive authority.

- The colour of a star directly depends on its size and surface temperature. In astronomy, the bigger a star, the hotter and brighter it is, and hotter and bigger stars are often blue in colour. Some blue stars may have hints of white and are considered to be extremely fiery and more ferocious than the reddish or yellowish stars.
Smaller stars like our sun are less bright and cooler than bigger stars. They are also reddish, yellowish or orangey in colour.

Contrary to the studies of stars in astronomy, a reddish, yellowish and orangey glow of fire on planet earth is known to be more livid than a blue glow of fire. In fact, a cooler glow of fire on earth is blue in colour and known as flames (e.g. gas cooker flames).

In the Scriptures, one of the notable names of God the Father is *Consuming Fire* (and fire is red on earth and not blue). In comparison, our earthly description of fire is identical with the colour of our sun, which represents the Father God.
Deuteronomy 4:24 and Hebrews 12:29 attributes the name 'Consuming fire' only to the Father.

- It has been confirmed by astronomers that the sun does not rotate as a solid at its exterior. The layers of the sun have been known to exhibit differential rotations. For example, at the equator, the sun's surface rotates once every 25.4 days, and near the poles, it rotates once every 36 days. This differential rotation extends considerably to the sun's interior. While the outer body of the sun does not appear solid, the core of the sun has been confirmed to be solid. The stark contrast in the astrophysical characteristics and motion of the sun is similar to the description of the Father in the scriptures.

In John 4:23–24, Jesus describes the Father to a certain Samaritan woman as a 'Spirit', which suggests that the Father is not flesh and bones like we are – just like the outer layers of the sun indicates. However, in Exodus 33:18–23, when Moses asked to see God face to face, God showed Moses his hands and back. This suggests that God owns a physical form as well. And just as we would need to travel into the depths of the sun to feel and touch its tangible form, we are advised in the scriptures that we cannot physically meet God in person until life after death.

Also, the book of Psalms 104:1–2a (KJV) adds: *'Bless the lord, O my soul. O Lord my God, thou art very great; thou art clothed with honour and majesty:* **who covers yourself with light as with a garment.***'* In comparison to the Father, the sun has a sub-surface of semi-solid iron beneath its non-solid photosphere (the photosphere is the visible surface of the sun, which we are familiar with and can see with our naked eyes - **the sun itself is actually hidden**). The brightness of the sun's photosphere is so overwhelming that it floods out both its core and even its chromosphere (chromosphere is the atmosphere and top layer above the photosphere).

Similarly, Psalm 104:2a reveals: *he covers himself with light as a garment*. Isaiah 45:15a also informs: *'Verily thou art a God that hideth thyself...'*

- It is impossible to physically visit the sun like humans have physically visited the moon. The only way possible for humans to directly approach the sun is by death. Likewise, God the Father said to Moses in Exodus 33:20 that no man could see his face and live. However, he permitted Moses to see his back as he walked at a large distance, just like a layman or the travelling astronomer could only view the sun at a far distance.

- Hydrogen is the fuel of the sun and converts into helium through the process of nuclear fusion as the sun ages. Both hydrogen and helium gases head the gas group in the sun. Though hydrogen has the least mass of all elements in the sun and helium has the second least mass of all elements, they are together the most abundant chemical elements in the sun. Hydrogen constitutes almost three quarters of our sun's mass, while helium constitutes a quarter of the sun, leaving less than two per cent of the sun's mass consisting of heavier elements like carbon, neon, oxygen, nitrogen, iron and silicon.

Characterised as the lightest of all gas elements in the sun, one may question how it is that hydrogen and helium make up 98 per cent of the sun.

This empirical information further illuminates Jesus' description of the Father as a Spirit. Light is often associated with the ethereal, and a lighter weight of air is also affiliated with the characteristics of a spirit! A clumsy example to illustrate this view is when a person gets light-headed from drinking spirits (alcohol). In several English dictionaries, a spirit is synonymous with light in terms of weight and also compared to gases as opposed to solid and liquid.

Also, a spirit is often characterised as a bodiless or airy entity that inhabits a place, object or persons. Similarly, our sun is inhabited by hydrogen and helium. It is as though the sun itself is a spirit.

Further, the sun is also 'a light' as it is light in weight. And though its chief components of hydrogen and helium are the lightest of gases, yet the sun is simultaneously the heaviest volume of mass in our solar system - just like the Biblical portrait of the Father God.

- Astronomers' comparison of our sun with other stars in the universe is fitly compatible with the biblical paradigm of the Father and the Holy Spirit. 1st Corinthians 2:10–11 states: *But God* [the Father] *hath revealed them to us by his Spirit* [Holy Spirit] *for the Spirit* [Holy Spirit] *searcheth all things, yes, the deep things of God* [the Father]. *For what man knoweth the things of a man, save the spirit of man which is in him? Even so the things of God* [the Father] *knoweth no man, but the Spirit of God* [Holy Spirit]'.

  As the Holy Spirit is capable of revealing intimate things about the Father God to us, according to the Bible, similarly, astronomers have acquired a greater understanding of our sun by examining the stars. They have witnessed supernovas – the death of stars and its formation process, which has significantly contributed to their understanding of the sun.

- The scriptures can be read in a dispensational context according to Bible theologians. Subsequently, the dispensation of the triune deity originates with the Father, the Son and then, the Holy Ghost. Similarly, our sun is first mentioned before the moon, and the moon before the stars in the Bible (Genesis 1:14).

In correlation, the Father is first revealed in the scriptures, then Jesus – just as the moon is secondary to the sun and cannot be luminous without the sun. Finally, the stars in the galaxies are furthest away from our planet, just as the Holy Ghost is the third person of the trinity that is revealed in the scriptures (Acts 2:1–4).

- The sun always appears to stand alone as the light giver during day. Correlatively, the book of James 1:17 describe the Father as the Father of all lights who has no tolerance for darkness – just as night is absent when the sun is out. There may be shades for cooling temperatures or one's shadow but that's about it. Every entity, person or thing 'directly' under the sun reflects its light and this is unlike the moon and stars at night. Also, when the sun is out, it appears to conceal the identities of the moon and stars. The sun seldom exhibits its close relationship with the moon and other stars in its executive position and leadership role; much like the characteristics of the Father in the Old Testament. Nonetheless, we can sometimes observe the moon in the sky during day, like the occasional visitations of Jesus in the Old Testament, before his descent to earth in human flesh.

- Bible critics often question why it is that the Father's voice and character appears to be louder and bolder than Jesus and the Holy Spirit, if indeed, the others are members of the Godhead. They insist that the Father's divinity is more obvious than the Son and the Holy Spirit.

  However, the astrophysical characteristics of the sun, moon and stars illuminate the revelation behind this mystery if we study its parody of the triune deity.

  Though stars in the universe share a similar nature to the sun, they are further from the earth, and the moon - though geographically closer to our planet than the sun - is quieter and dim. Subsequently, the Father's voice 'appears' to be the loudest in the scriptures, just like the brighter luminosity of our sun during day.

  Despite the sun being further from earth than the moon, it is more lucid and vivid to notice and observe. Also, just as sunlight on the moon is more predictable than the planet earth, Christ Jesus remains a closer deity to humanity.

  In fact, the three world major monotheists: Judaism, Islam and Christianity, who believe in the worship of one God all await the coming of Jesus Christ and not the Father God (Selah)! While some believe this to be Christ's second coming, others believe this will be his first.

- Without the mediating position and function of the moon between the earth and sun, the sun may seem overpowering and overwhelming to planet earth. If the sun is left alone with planet earth, it is likely to exert excessive gravitational pull on our planet. However, our moon evens the odds of any potential catastrophe of this sort and maintains a friendly balance between the two. It is this balance that allows planet earth to enjoy all its lifelong goodness and benefits from our sun. We could have missed out on photosynthesis, which gives light and energy to our plants and plants in turn provides oxygen, food and habitation for animals and humans. Also, liquid water is available because of the sun's presence, and it is liquid water that is responsible for the emergence of all life forms. The sun also provides substantial heat in maintaining regular body temperatures and helps with evaporation, which in turn causes rain to fall for farming. Vitamin D and solar energy for electronics are also benefits from the sun.

Though the sun often looks boisterous and intimidating, yet it provides more benefits for the survival of life on our planet than the moon. And most certainly, it is the moon that helps us realise these benefits. In comparison, the scripture reveals that the Father is greater than the *son of man*. Genesis 1:16: *'And God made two great lights; the greater light* [i.e. Sun] *to rule the day, and the lesser light* [i.e. moon] *to rule the night…'* John 14:28b adds: *'I* [Jesus] *go to my Father; for my Father is greater than I.'*

- Astronomers have confirmed that the sun often emits extremely charged particles (mostly electrons and protons) known as the solar wind, which travels through the solar system. King David expressed God's anger with a similar description to the fiery sun: *'Thou shalt make them as a fiery oven in the time of thine anger: the LORD shall swallow them up in his wrath, and the fire shall devour them'* (Psalms 21:9).

However, the sun has also been confirmed by astronomers to have speckles of many spots, known as sun spots. These spots emerge when dense bundles of magnetic field lines from the interior of the sun break through its surface, and would often vary as its solar magnetic activity (a process known as the solar cycle). The sun spots are confirmed to be the cooler region of the sun's surface. Correlatively, this empirical information illustrates that the fiery and angry-looking sun possess in its nature a staying flow of kindness, much like the Father's loving kindness and tender mercies. The scriptures confirms this in Psalm 103:8–9 *'The Lord is merciful and gracious, slow to anger, and plenteous in mercy. He will not always chide: neither will he keep his anger forever.'*

Furthermore, the helium present in the sun is a safe and non-flammable gas used as a cooling medium for nuclear reactors - like hydrogen, which is also in the sun. Helium, existing as one of the chief components of the sun further illustrates the sun's kind and cool nature. In fact, as the sun ages, its hydrogen component converts to helium. And unlike hydrogen, helium does not burn!

Helium is also the non-flammable gas we often use to fill party balloons; and like some Americans would say – 'There is fun in the sun, y'all!' I agree. The sun is where the party's at, but first, we'll need a celestial body if we are to take that literally. Helium is often associated with humour and a mouthful of it can make one's voice sound really funny. These revelations imply that God does have a sense of humour (Psalms 2:4); or where do we think we got ours from?

Jesus' first miracle in the scriptures was at a wedding party, where he turned water to wine. And though the wine tasted different, the guests at the wedding remarked that

Jesus' wine was exceptionally good. This meant that Jesus knew how to host a party (John 1:1–11).

Like the Father in the Old Testament, Jesus knew how to celebrate good times. There are several festive feasts in the Bible - Passover feasts, the feast of unleavened bread, the feast of first fruits, Shavuot/Pentecost feasts, the feast of trumpets, Yom Kippur feast e.t.c. The Old Testament consists of many festive occasions. Even at the arrival of the third person of the trinity – the Holy Ghost - the apostles appeared to behave like drunkards, and had to explain to the public that they were not drunk but filled with the spirit (Acts 2:13–18). Ecclesiastes 10:19 illuminates: *'A __feast__ is made for laughter __and wine__ maketh merry...'*

Surprisingly, the ending glory and final remains of the sun will be helium – just like the biblical portrait of heaven's rejoicing and feastings awaiting the saints in heaven, and like this famous quote I like - 'He who laughs last laughs longest' - taken from the old proverb from Tudor England, and was first performed in Cambridge around 1608: *'Laugh on, laugh on my friend, hee laugheth best that laugheth to the end.'*

THE STARS

*'There is **one** glory of the sun, and another* [one] *glory of the moon, and another **glory of the stars: for one star differeth from another star in glory'***

- 1 Corinthians 15:41

Astronomers and theologians both agree the earth has one sun and one moon. However, in comparison to the sun and moon, stars are many in number and would seem more intricate to communicate individually.

Before God the Father uttered his first words in Genesis 1:3, the Holy Spirit had pioneered the creation stage by his melodious movement. Who is the Holy Spirit? Furthermore, who is the Holy Ghost??

The subject of the Holy Ghost is about the bond and union created by the life of Christ (i.e. Jesus' resurrected life) and the Holy Spirit. Though the Holy Spirit is the third person of the trinity, the Holy Spirit is not entirely the Holy Ghost. It is

Jesus, who was raised from the dead (as a ghost) by the Holy Spirit (Romans 8:11a) that collectively and symbiotically constitutes the eminent Holy Ghost. Subsequently, stars represent Jesus' resurrected life as Christ and the Holy Spirit as well. Also, stars are used in the narratives of the scriptures to represent other celestial beings and persons (we will understand the reason for this as we continue reading).

- The births of stars ensue from the same path to their death. Colossians 1:18b expressly states that Jesus was born from the dead. This statement 'born from the dead' may not make much sense in everyday living. However, farmers understand the semantics of this kind from their line of trade, as they often practice burying lifeless seeds, which are acquired from the life of a previous tree or plant to create another tree or plant.

  The same is true in the story of the birth and death of stars. Every star experiences death prior to its birth, which means that each stars experience death at least twice in its lifetime. In the case of an older star that's reborn, a star will experience death thrice. According to the astronomic story for the evolution of stars, it is said by astronomers that a giant cloud of gas and dust is first hit by a density or shock wave, which results in a gravitational disintegration of the concentrated clouds. As gravity shrinks the clouds, it becomes hotter in the middle until a nuclear reaction occurs. This nuclear reaction creates a resistance against the force of gravity and consequently, ignites a newborn star.

With older stars that have already lived a full life, most of their nuclear energy has been converted to helium so they may not have enough hydrogen fuel to generate adequate nuclear reactions to resist the force of gravity; in which case, gravity will utterly take over the potential star formation process and obliterate the star's opportunity to live again.

It is the balance achieved between the pressure of heat resistance against the force of gravity that ignites a star and maintains its life cycle. If this balance is lost, the light of a star will diminish. Therefore, gravity is just as important as the nuclear reactions activities in the formation of a star.

In correlation to the scriptures, the symbolic narrative of death before the birth of stars sheds a radiant light on the subject of Jesus as one who was born from the dead (and on the subject of being born again). Many have questioned how it is possible for an embodiment of divinity to experience death. Some have even ridiculed the story of Jesus' death and resurrection as something beneath God's intelligence and theirs. Certainly, it is below and above us but not beneath God's intelligence – we can see it in agriculture and in the cosmos.

Just as many years of agriculture have sustained humanity, the stars above long preceded the existence of humanity.

Before the acquired knowledge of astrophysics and astrodynamics and before the knowledge of astronomy was uncovered by humans, the scripture had already revealed that Jesus, the second person of the Holy Trinity, was born from the dead. And today we can see that this witness is true. Stars (a symbol of Christ) are **literally** born from the dead!

- Acts 2:1–4 records the event of the first visit of the Holy Ghost to the early church: *'And when the day of Pentecost was fully come, they were all with one accord in one place. And suddenly there came a sound from heaven as of a rushing mighty wind, and it filled all the house where they were sitting. And there appeared unto them cloven tongues like as of fire, and it sat upon each of them. And they were all filled with the Holy Ghost, and began to speak with other tongues, as the Spirit gave them utterance.'* Prior to the manifested cloven tongues of fire, the scriptures state that a sound of a rushing mighty wind was present. Similarly, in astronomy, a sudden shockwave coupled with a concentrated interstellar wind of gas and dust initiates the birth of a star. Also, stars that are newly born are identified by the ignition of a burning fire, just like the cloven tongues of fire that appeared on the day of Pentecost. If the Holy Ghost was represented by the sun, this verse of scripture would have recorded one manifested cloven tongue of fire. However, because the Holy Ghost is represented by stars, more than one emblem of fire (i.e. stars) was present in the visitation of the Holy Ghost to the early Church.

- Stars are often found in clusters, just like the manifestation of the Holy Spirit in scriptures. Isaiah 11:2 from the Old Testament records: *'And the spirit of the LORD shall rest upon him, the spirit of wisdom and understanding, the spirit of counsel and might, the spirit of knowledge and of the fear of LORD.'* And 1 Corinthians 12:4–11 from the New Testament records: *'Now there are diversities of gifts but the same spirit. And there are differences of administrations, but the same lord. And there are diversities of operations but it is the same God which worketh all in all. But the manifestation of the spirit is giving to every man to profit withal. For to one is given by the spirit, the word of wisdom; to another the word of knowledge by the same spirit; to another faith by the same spirit; to another the gift of* healing by the same spirit; to another the workings of miracles; to another prophecy; to another discerning of spirits; to another diverse kinds of tongues; to another the interpretation of tongues: But all these worketh **that one and the same selfsame spirit**, dividing to every man severally as he will.'

- According to astronomers, the process of a star formation is preceded by the movement of a shockwave or density wave. However, astronomers have not been able to ascertain where this movement comes from. Jesus said the following in John 3:8: *'The wind bloweth where listeth and thou hearest the sound thereof, but canst not tell whence it cometh, and whither it goeth: so is every one that is born of the Spirit.'*

- The function of stars is similar to the moon: they both give light at night. Like the union of Jesus and the Holy Spirit, the moon and the stars work as a pair. In John 15:26, Jesus said: *'But when the Comforter is come, whom I will send to you from the Father, even **the Spirit of truth**, who proceedeth out of the Father, he **shall testify of me**.'* Similarly, stars can assist the moon in providing light during night. John 14:26 also adds: *'But the Comforter which is the Holy Ghost, whom the Father will send in my name, he shall teach you all things and bring all things to your remembrance, whatsoever I said unto you.'* Again,

Jesus' words allegorically state that stars, which are symbolic of the sun (that represents the Father), can create an awareness for the moon and add to its visibility. Also, it is unlikely that we view the stars at night without remembering the moon.

- Because stars symbolise the Holy Ghost, they also represent the church of Christ, which are alternatively referred to as the body of Jesus Christ (Ephesians 5:23). Though Jesus was sent to the world and belongs to the world (John 3:16), the Holy Ghost is sent 'exclusively' to the Church of Jesus and not the world (John 14:17). Subsequently, the primary difference between the church and the world is not Jesus but the Holy Ghost.

As it is that Jesus' identity in the scriptures has always been dual, Jesus ('Yeshua' in Hebrew) was his name from birth and the name he answered to, but 'Christ' was the divine name revealed to Peter, a name that Jesus bore before his descent to earth in human flesh (John 1:14). This is the reason Jesus said to Peter that there was no way he could have understood who he was as the Christ, except the Father had revealed this to Peter (Matthew 16:13–20). Jesus also revealed in the scriptures that he was the long awaited

'Christ' while speaking to a Samaritan woman in John 4:25–26.

As 'Jesus' being the birth name of Yeshua, Jesus is represented by the moon, and the moon represents his life before death, and his identity as the seed of promise from the loins of father Abraham. However, his identity as 'Christ' correlates with the stars. And the stars represent Jesus' resurrected life after death and his identity as a co-founder of the Church (Holy "Ghost") and the bridegroom of the church in the age to come (Ephesians 5:25).

This dual identity of 'Jesus' and 'Christ' is the reason other religions and the secular world may identify Jesus as a good person and great teacher but nothing more (i.e. earth and moon-like). It is also the reason the Church could recognise Jesus as the divine Christ (i.e. sun and star-like). It is evident that the world knows of 'Jesus' but not everything there is to know. However, those who believe in Jesus' divinity and resurrection from the dead realise his true identity and are, by biblical definition, his Church and bride.

1st Corinthians 12:3b sheds more light: *'And that no man can say that Jesus is the lord,* **but by the Holy Ghost'**. In other words, it is the Holy Ghost, represented by stars, who makes it possible for a person to willingly acknowledge the lordship of Jesus. Without the Holy Ghost, our perception of Jesus will be terrestrial - like the earth and dim like the moon. However, like stars, the Holy Ghost helps us realise that Jesus is so much more.

Furthermore, compared to other moons in our solar system, forensic astronomy speculates that the formation of the earth's moon was through the process of decimation. A similar account is also proposed for the stars. These similarities reveal a cogent and consistent kinship between the astronomical narrative of our moon and stars' origin, just as Jesus 'the Christ' professed to be both a son of man and the son of God.

- *'And I saw no temple therein: for the **Lord God Almighty** and the **Lamb** are the temple of it. And the city had no need of the **sun**, neither of the **moon**, to shine in it: for the glory of God* [the Father] *did lighten it, and the Lamb is the light thereof* [the Son, like the moon].*' –* Revelation 21:22-23.

It is interesting to find that this text compares the functions of the sun and moon to the Father and Son. Evidently, the insights shared in this book may seem complicated but they are not fabricated. Furthermore, these verses mirror Jesus as a lamb in comparison to the moon, which symbolises Jesus' sacrifice and death at the cross. However, in the next chapter and verse, Jesus revealed himself as a star, which symbolises his resurrection: *'I, Jesus have sent mine angel to testify unto you these things in the churches. **I am** the root and offspring of David, and **the bright and morning star.'** -* Revelations 22:16. These two texts further confirm that the moon and stars are symbolic of Jesus' dual identity.

There are obvious similarities between the sun and stars, much like the Father and the Holy Spirit (John 4:24) but similarities between the moon and stars are not as obvious. As Jesus (represented by the moon) is a chief component of the Holy **Ghost**, we will find that evidences for the Holy **Ghost** can also be seen in the characteristics of our moon.

After Jesus' resurrection from the dead, the scriptures record that his ghostly presence permeates the Christian heart. However, many sceptics think this is preposterous. They ask questions like – how is it possible that someone who is long dead and gone continues to be present with us. And also question that even if such a person was supernaturally resurrected from the dead, and has both physically **and spiritually** gone to heaven, how is it possible that they continue to be present on earth? Even a departed human soul is incapable of this phenomenon. However, the mystery of Jesus' ghostly omnipresence can be seen in the astrophysical behaviour of our moon.

Any astronomer will stress that the moon is as dead as a doorknob; but somehow, gravity keeps the moon close to earth every minute and second of the day. The moon's behaviour is so predictable and reliable that it is as dependable as the living. There has been no substantial evidence to confirm a meteorological, biological and geological activity on the moon. And if we were to examine the moon solely from its astrophysical characteristic (i.e. its internal activity), without considering its distance to planet earth, we will find that the moon descriptively resembles a ghost. It is dead, yet living. **It is a ghost that orbits the rotating earth!**

Further, some avid readers of this book may ask: 'If the moon is a symbol of a ghost (i.e. the Holy Ghost), wouldn't this contradict with the proposition that the moon is also a symbol of the life of Jesus before his death?' The answer here is a yes and no.

Before Jesus' death, he lived in total submission to his Father's will. In John 4:34, Jesus confessed that his food was to do the will of the Father. And in John 5:30, he also said: *'I cannot do anything of myself but as I hear I judge…'*

Prior to Jesus' birth, he was described by the angel Gabriel as a progeny of the Holy Ghost, which implies that his death and resurrection was inevitably predetermined before his human birth – Luke 1:34–35.

Like Jesus, his true followers barely own their life. In a sense, they are already living martyrs, having already given their lives to Jesus (2 Corinthians 4:11). When the apostle Paul reflected on his spiritual journey with Jesus, he confessed: *'I die daily.'* (1 Corinthians 15:31b). Also, John the Baptist, long before the death of Jesus, referred to him as the Lamb of God who takes away the sins of the world (John 1:29).

In John 14:17, the scripture implicitly concedes how the moon could represent Jesus' life before and after his death. In this verse, Jesus spoke to his disciples (prior to his death) about the coming Holy Spirit: *'And I will pray to the father, and he shall give you another comforter that may abide with you forever; even the spirit of truth; whom the world cannot receive,* *because the world seeth him not, neither knoweth him: but **you know him**; for he* [presently] *dwelleth with you, and shall* [later] *be in you.'* (Selah).

There is a thin line between the living dead and a dead man living; they sound alike but they are not the same. The living dead are what Hollywood movies call zombies, and the dead men living are what Hollywood movies call ghosts! It's not much of a change; it's what I like to call an interchange. Yes, the moon has been the same for ages, but if you look real closely, it's not quite the same.

- It is widely known that stars are located outside our solar system. However, if we are looking at the solar system from an extra-solar planet, or happen to live in another planetary system (e.g. Kepler-11 planetary system), the sun would seem like a star as well. Because of life on earth, we know the sun is not another star. However, from the distant view of other planetary systems, it would seem so. Similarly, the myriad presence of stars in the galactic cosmos symbolically correlates with the biblical record of the omnipresent God. Psalms 139:7 reveals: *'Whither shall I go from thy spirit? Or whither shall I flee from thy presence? If I ascend up into heaven, thou art there: If I make my bed in hell, behold, thou art there.'* In this verse, the psalmist directly addresses the Father (who is

86

represented by the sun), but is indirectly speaking of his Spirit (who is represented by the stars). Though the Father himself is a spirit (John 4:24), he has another spirit, who is the Holy Spirit. Unlike humans, who are spirits of flesh, the Father is both a spirit of spirits (Hebrews 12:9), and a Spirit of the Spirit.

Another verse of scripture that illuminates verse 7 in Psalm 139 is Psalm 51:11, where David prayed: *'Cast me not away from Your presence; and do not take Your **Holy Spirit** from me.'* It is not the Father who is omnipresent, but the spirit of the Father, who is the Holy Spirit. However, because the spirit of the Father (Holy Spirit) is never without the Father, the Father is also omnipresent! The Son has been seen (Revelation 1:13-16), the Father also has been seen (Exodus 33:20-23), but who has seen the Holy Spirit in like manner? The Holy Spirit is the omnipresent component of the Holy Trinity, as hundreds of billions of stars in the vast cosmos illustrates.

- Stars are known to exist at a distance and often appear as dots in the sky because of their vast distance. Symbolically, where stars are first mentioned in the scriptures, the sun and moon were previously mentioned. Genesis 1:16: *'And God made two great lights; the greater light* [sun] *to rule the day, and the lesser light* [moon] *to rule the night: he made the stars also.'*

Correlatively, the Father is the first of the Holy Trinity that's revealed in the scriptures, and the Son is the second. Presently, we are living in the dispensation of the Holy Ghost, which is the chief reason the New Testament often describes the days of the church as the last days (Acts 2:17, 1 Timothy 4:1).

Considering the moon is both terrestrial (earthly) and extra-terrestrial (sun-like), and stars are purely celestial, those who dwell at a far distance from the terrestrial, like the celestial angels and the resurrected saints, are also represented by stars.

In Job 38:7, God described the angels as stars: *'When the* **morning stars** *sang together, and all* **the sons of God** *shouted for joy.'* Also, Lucifer, who was once a star, is depicted in the scriptures as a falling star (Revelation 9:1). Additionally, in Revelations 2:25–28, Jesus encouraged his Church to endure to the very end so they can receive a morning star:

'And he that overcometh, and keepeth my works unto the end, to him will I give power over the nations: And he shall rule them with a rod of iron; as the vessels of a potter, shall they be broken

into shivers: even as I received of my Father. **And I will give him the morning star.'**

It is often at the end of a saint's journey that the promise of a morning star is delivered to them. Matthew 22:30 also confirms that the bridal Church of Jesus at her resurrection will be like the angels of heaven, which are the morning stars (Job 38:7).

Furthermore, according to John 1:12, those who receive Jesus are 'becoming' sons of God, they are not quite there yet! And the reason for this gradual progression is because we begin our journey with Jesus on the level of the moon – which is partly terrestrial and partly extra-terrestrial. However, as we grow in our knowledge of Jesus, we become purged and transformed into the heavenly image of him, just like the morning star - which is purely celestial.

We may never attain the full height (of the celestial) while living in our unglorified bodies. In fact, God may not permit us to. He may give us glimpses of the celestial glory from time to time, but would not permit a total transition of such, while we live on earth. If he did, our purpose on earth as humans would have to be terminated. We would cease to be relevant to earth if we take on the full body of the celestial, in which case, it will be better to join the angels in heaven and cohabitate with them.

Nonetheless, the scriptures encourage us to excel in our knowledge of Christ Jesus once we receive him in our hearts (Colossians 3:2). There is undoubtedly a greater reward from God for those who pursue a deeper relationship with him.

2 Timothy 2:19–21 sheds more light: *'Nevertheless the foundation of God standeth sure, having this seal; The Lord knoweth them that are his. And, let every one that nameth the name of Christ depart from iniquity. But in a great house there are not only vessels of gold* [i.e. sun-like and star-like, yellow and white gold] *and of silver* [moon-like], *but also of wood and of earth* [these are the carnal and terrestrial kind]; ... *some to honour, and some to dishonor. If a man therefore purges himself from these, he shall be a vessel unto honor, sanctified, and meet for the master's use and prepared unto every good work.'*

This Biblical text advises that we should strive to progress from the earth level to the moon level and from the moon level to the star level.

Also, Daniel 12:3 adds: *'And they that be wise shall <u>shine as the brightness of the firmament</u>: and they that turn many to righteousness <u>as the stars forever and ever.</u>'*

Notice that 'forever and ever' in this verse of scripture is associated with 'stars'. Figuratively, a moon can grow into a star some day and bring others into the light as well. However, every transition from the ground level is made possible with the help and guidance of the Holy Ghost. Romans 8:14 states: *'For as many are led by the Spirit of God, they are the sons of God* ('sons of God' are alternatively known as 'morning stars' in relation to angels).

It is the Holy Ghost that guides and reconciles the conflicting identities of the terrestrial and extra-terrestrial within the followers of Christ, who are called to shine as the lights of Jesus in the world, just like the moon at night.

It is also the Holy Ghost who is the star guide that appoints, determines and manages every son of God, including the morning stars that the book of Job describes as angels. This is the reason why ALL STARS in heaven represent the Holy Ghost (whether angels, resurrected saints or the soon-to-be-resurrected)! Finally, 1 John 3:2–3 declares:

'Beloved, now are we the sons of God, and it doth not yet appear what we shall be; but we know that when He shall appear, we shall be like Him; for we shall see Him as He is. And every man

that hath this hope in him purifieth himself even as He is pure.' (Selah)

- Stars are the celestial symbol of the Holy Spirit, who is also the Holy Ghost. For us, stars are essentially about Christ Jesus. The scriptures states in Colossians 2:9–10: *'For in him* [Jesus Christ] *dwells the fullness of the Godhead bodily. And you are complete in him, who is the head of all principality and power.'*

John 16:13–14 advises that the primary purpose of the Holy Spirit is to glorify Jesus and not himself. Just as Jesus glorified the Father, the Holy Spirit's primary purpose is to glorify Jesus: and this is the trinity code. Each member of the Holy Trinity is committed to serve and esteem the will of the other.

One other reason it appears that stars symbolise Christ Jesus rather than the Holy Spirit is because Jesus can be known in the flesh and spirit, as we are flesh and spirit, but the Holy Spirit, as his name implies, can only be known in spirit! Sadly, some of us will only understand the Holy Spirit better in heaven than here on earth. For now, Jesus is the exemplary prototype of stars (which represents the Holy Spirit). And as Jesus is before all creation, and a first-born before the saints of old, today and tomorrow (Romans 8:29b and Colossians 1:15), every heavenly angel was created to have Jesus' spirit and body, and every heavenly saint was created to have his spirit, soul and body. Though we may look like Jesus when we arrive in heaven, he is the first star among many. He is the original and we were made in his likeness. Angels and the resurrected saints are star-like, but Jesus is the star!

To the carnal mind, it is preposterous and difficult to think a human can be divine, but to the spiritual mind, God can be as small as he is big, because he is God after all, and all things – both small and big, were created by him. The real struggle in embracing the divinity of Christ has to do with our preconceived ideas and notions of a God that we have never seen. No human knows for certain what God looks like.

Even those who have encountered God have only seen a mirror or reflection of him. Whether we believe in the divinity of Jesus or not, he is the best example of the unseen God. Jesus loved humanity more than any other. He forgave those who wounded and crucified him mercilessly. His birth defied the law of reproduction and biology, his first miracle defied the laws of fermentation and chemistry, his ascension to heaven defied the law of gravity and physics, his miracles of healing the sick defied the law of medicine, and his resurrection from the dead defied death. He must be God.

In Revelation 1:16, the scriptures compare him to the sun (symbol of the Father). In Revelation 21:23, the scriptures compare him to the moon (symbol of the Son). In Revelation 22:16, the scriptures compare him to the stars (symbol of the Holy Ghost).

But what did Jesus actually say about his divine nature? One may ask. Did he ever claim to be divine? According to Matthew 1:1 and many other Biblical texts, Jesus is the descendant of Abraham and David. However, on certain occasions, Jesus purposely contradicted his earthly ties with David and Abraham to reveal his pre-existent identity as the divine. In Revelation 22:16, Jesus said: *'I am the root and the offspring of David, and the bright morning star'*. This means he was before David and yet came after David in human flesh. Matthew 22:41–46 expounds: *'While the Pharisees were gathered together, Jesus asked them, saying, "What do you think about the Christ? Whose Son is He?" They said to Him, "The Son of David." He said to them, "How then does David in the*

Spirit call Him 'Lord,' saying: 'The Lord said to my Lord, "Sit at My right hand, till I make Your enemies Your footstool"? If David then calls Him 'Lord,' how is He his Son?" And no one was able to answer Him a word, nor from that day on did anyone dare question Him anymore.'

Also, in John 8:56–58, Jesus contradicted his earthly relation to Abraham: *'Your father Abraham rejoiced to see my day: and he saw it and was glad. Then the Jews said to him, Thou art not yet 50 years old, and hast thou seen Abraham? Jesus said unto them, Verily, verily, I say unto you, before Abraham was, I am.'*

According to Jesus, not only did Abraham meet with him, but he admits that he was before Abraham - *'Before Abraham was, **I am**'*, means he was not just before Abraham; he is and has always been present. *'I am'* here suggests that he has no past or future, he just is! This was the same response that God the Father gave to Moses in Exodus 3:13–14:

'And Moses said unto God, Behold when I come unto the children of Israel, and shall say unto them, the God of your fathers hath sent me unto you; and they shall say to me, What is his name? what shall I say unto them? And God said unto Moses, I AM THAT I AM: and he said, Thus shalt thou say unto the children of Israel, I AM hath sent me unto you.'

Evidently, Jesus appears to speak in the same manner as the Father did with Moses.

Furthermore, the celestial symbol of stars introduced the birth of Jesus and also marked his resurrected life after death. According to Matthew 2:1–11, a star led certain wise men from the Far East to find baby Jesus (for the purpose of worshipping him and presenting him with gifts).

This star indicates that he was of celestial origin and did not need to be born in the palaces of kings to confirm the existence of his eternal kingdom. Also, at his resurrection, Jesus walked through closed doors, disappeared, re-appeared and moved faster than the speed of light (Mark 16:14, John 20:26). Jesus even ascended into heaven on two separate occasions (as shown in John 20:16–17 and Acts 1:9–10).

As a child, I remember I use to think Superman was real; I even thought I'd fly like him some day; now I know that's possible! Do you remember the story of Philip (from the chapter on the moon)? Philip was the disciple who challenged Jesus to show him and the other disciples, the Father (in John 14:7–9). Philip was so eager to experience this pure celestial realm but couldn't, because Jesus had not yet been resurrected (i.e. universally revealed to be more than human or glorified!). Guess what later happened to Philip after Jesus' resurrection?

Acts 8:39-40 narrates: *'And when they were come up out of water, the spirit of the lord caught away Philip, that the eunuch*

saw him no more: and he went on his way rejoicing. Philip was
found at Azotus: and passing through he preached in all the cities,
till he came to Caesarea.'

Can you see this? Philip travelled just like Jesus did after his resurrection. Like angels would! Tennessee Williams once said that *'Time is the longest distance between two places'*. Certainly, this did not apply to the flight of Philip. Prophets in scriptures mentally and spiritually time-travelled to the past or future, but Philip 'physically' time travelled! God is full of pleasant surprises and can certainly exceed our expectations.

Philip's story is an extraordinary witness of a prayer-answering God! Normally, God reserves this kind of experience for saints on their way to heaven, like in the stories of Enoch and Elijah, who ascended to heaven, or the dead and buried saints of old who also ascended into heaven after the resurrection of Jesus (Matthew 27:52). But Philip was the only human in the scriptures who experienced this extraordinary means of transportation on earth without the formal requirement to ascend into heaven. The apostle Paul described this space-time travel experience as having 'the glorious body' (Philippians 3:20–21).

A BIT PERSONAL

- In the year 2010, on the 19th of May I did something I never thought possible. It was a Wednesday and a late afternoon. I knelt on my bathroom floor and said a prayer to God to provide some sort of financial miracle so I could self-publish a memoir I had previously written. I was struggling financially, frustrated and exhausted because all my efforts to succeed had seemed in vain. While passionately praying to God, I thought I heard a voice say to me to give a specific amount for the purpose of promoting the gospel of Christ Jesus. Because I'm accustomed to giving to God's work and charities, it didn't bother me at first. In fact, I continued praying. But as I later gathered my thoughts and tried to make sense of the amount I heard, I realised that this amount was approximately all I had in my bank account.

I couldn't understand this. Was it God speaking? How could God expect me to give all I had saved, especially at a time when I felt so vulnerable and was asking for a financial miracle? It didn't make any sense whatsoever. I have always given to the cause of the gospel and it wasn't new for me to give sacrificially to God's work or charities, but this time was different: the money was all I had.

However, I knew deep within that it was God speaking to me. I had not imagined the amount, I heard it instinctively, and it so happened to be what I had in my bank account. I also knew I could not smother the voice that spoke to me or pretend that I did not hear it. My conscience was stirred and I had a conviction to obey.

Though it was a lot to give away and was not the best time to do so in my reasoning, I knew if I did not obey God's voice immediately, I would not have done so later. I didn't want to think about it and wanted to get it over with quickly. So I dashed to my house phone to make the call to honour the transaction. I cried as I picked up the phone. I called a particular church ministry whose commitment to God's work I strongly believed in. My heart was broken, with tears streaming down my face; I quietly cried all through our dialogue on the phone while giving my account details to the representative of this church ministry. I remember the gentleman I spoke to was so quick in taking my card details that it felt like I was being robbed. I later realised that God had asked me to give all the money I had saved because of what it meant to me. It could have been anything else that meant something to me but by giving

God all I had in that present moment, I was giving him all my heart.

The next day and two days following, the voice of the Father visited me. During this visitation, I received the vision to write this second book, which you are now reading – 'The Ambassador of God'. The Father promised that there would be signs and wonders in the heavens (i.e. cosmos) and in the earth to pave the way for the message he had given me to share with the world.

The first sign in the heavens that he fulfilled in preparing the way for this message was the rare super moon on March 19th, 2011. Another outlandish sign for the moon was on June 15th, 2011 – the longest lunar eclipse in 100 years. These events and many other recent celestial and earthly events awakened society's consciousness in a unique way and created a more inquisitive need all over the world to learn about the extra-terrestrial sphere and to inquire more into the activities of our moon and other celestial objects.

In addition, another sign for stars was fulfilled on April 6th, 2011. (Please note that the death and crucifixion of Jesus, many years back, coincides with April 6th, a fact I discovered long after I'd finished writing this volume.)

On that day, as part of a survey conducted by the MMT observatory on Mount Hopkins, Ariz, astronomers discovered a pair of white dwarf stars whirling around each other every 39 minutes at a distance less than that of the moon from the earth. These stars, though near the end of their lives, were allegedly looking to enjoy a second life together. Astronomers proposed that in a few million years these stars will merge and reignite as one helium burning star. The fate of these stars is sealed for a rebirth.

White dwarf stars are dead or dying stars with sun-like matter. Stars that are not like our sun end their lives differently, e.g. as a neutron star or black hole. Normally, white dwarf stars collide and explode as a supernova, but these recently discovered stars have stunned astronomers because this is the first time in history they have witnessed this space phenomenon.

In addition, the discovered two dying stars are not identical. Only one of them is visible, and that one was expected to weigh more than the other, but actually weighs less. Because of this inconsistency, some students of astronomy have refuted the identity of the invisible star as a white dwarf. Some speculate that the obscured star may be a neutron star and others think it may be a brown dwarf or a black hole. More and more questions surround this subject as the authority of the astronomers who identified both stars seems to be undermined. However, the astronomers involved maintain that the discovered stars are both white dwarfs despite their odd differences. It is certainly evident that this discovery is unconventional.

Over several decades and centuries, the Bible has exhibited a timeless relevance to historic events. And as we will soon find here, the scriptures lends a vivid voice to the recently discovered white dwarfs, their symbolic meaning and a message we can extrapolate from its astronomic narrative.

Bible students are aware that the Holy Spirit, who worked alongside God the Father in the Old Testament, suddenly took another title as the Holy Ghost after Jesus' resurrection. So the biblical paradigm here is to relate the two white dwarfs and their emerging identity in the near future with the identities of Jesus, the Holy Spirit and the Holy Ghost.

After the resurrection and reunion of Jesus with his disciples in John 20:21–22, the scriptures state – *'Then said Jesus to them again, peace be unto you: as my Father hath sent me, even so*

I send you. And when he had said this, **he breathed on them, and said unto them, Receive the Holy Ghost.'** Genesis 2:7 illuminates the unique incidence between Jesus and his disciples: *'And the Lord God formed man out of the dust of the ground,* **and breathed into his nostrils the breath of life; and man became a living soul.'** Job 27:3 clarifies what the breath of life is: *'All the while* **my breath is in me, and the Spirit of God is in my nostrils.'**

From the above scriptures, it is clear that since the beginning of creation, the Holy Spirit has governed earthly matters with the Father, which is also long before the human birth of Jesus. Luke 1:34–35 indicates that a transition from Holy Spirit to the Holy Ghost was in motion before Jesus' birth. However, it was the death and resurrection of Jesus that officially established the new identity of the Holy Spirit as the Holy Ghost.

In comparison, the visible white dwarf that was recently discovered symbolically represents Jesus in human form, while the unseen white dwarf symbolically represents the Holy Spirit: the reason for this is because the Holy Spirit has no visible or physical form.

The full identity of the Holy Spirit is portrayed vividly in the Old Testament all through the dispensation of the Father and has certainly exceeded the 33 years duration of Jesus' identity in physical human form. Therefore, a celestial symbol of the Holy Spirit should appear voluminous and heavier – just like astronomers have confirmed that the unseen white dwarf weighs 43 per cent as much as the sun and the visible white dwarf weighs 17 per cent in comparison. Also, the discovery of the unseen white dwarf fits Jesus' announcement and description of the Holy Spirit's appearance. John 14:17: *'Even the spirit of truth: whom the world cannot receive, because the world seeth him not, neither knoweth him: but you know him; for he dwelleth with you, and shall be in you.'* This verse symbolically indicates that the world will struggle to identify the Holy Spirit and the transition of the Holy Spirit to the Holy Ghost.

Just as well, astronomers were able to identify the presence of the unseen white dwarf because they had previously examined the movements of the visible white dwarf around it. A press release from the Harvard–Smithsonian Centre for Astrophysics published on April 6th stated the following: *'The newly identified binary star (designated SDSS J010657.39 – 100003.3) is located about 7,800 light-years away in the constellation Cetus. It consists of **two white dwarfs, a visible star and an unseen companion whose presence is betrayed by the*** *visible star's motion around it.'* This publication, by astronomer Dr Mukremin Kilic, complements the words of Jesus in John 15:26–27: *'But when the Comforter* [Holy Spirit] *is come, whom I will send to you from the Father, **even the spirit of truth, who proceedeth from the Father, he shall testify of me and you also shall bear witness,** <u>**because you have been with me from the beginning.**</u>'*

Introspectively, Dr Kilic and his colleagues were able to discover the unseen white dwarf because they had first acknowledged the visible white dwarf.

In this similar vein, Dr Kilic and his colleagues are like the disciples of Jesus who had been with Jesus from the beginning (i.e. by first observing the visible star) and later testified of the Holy Spirit (which is the unseen star) and the Holy Ghost's upcoming transition (i.e. the new star waiting to be reborn from the union of both white dwarfs). In John 16:13–14, Jesus added: *'Howbeit when he, the Spirit of truth is come, he will guide you into all truth: **for he shall not speak of himself;** but whatsoever he shall hear, that shall he speak: **and he will show you things to come. He shall glorify me: for he shall receive of mine,** and shall show it to you'*. Here again, Jesus confirms that the Holy Spirit (before his transition to the Holy Ghost) will be inconspicuous - like the unseen star. He also said the Holy Spirit would come to show upcoming event(s) that are for the purpose of glorifying him. Verse 14 states: *'for he shall receive of mine'*, suggests that he (the Holy Spirit) is an independent individual who will take Jesus into himself, and *'shall show it to us'* suggests that the independent Holy Spirit will merge with Jesus to reveal more about Jesus.

Similarly, it is the visible white dwarf that will become more visible with the assistance of the unseen white dwarf. This is what Jesus allegorically expressed in this verse of scripture. The Holy Spirit will glorify him, just as the unseen star will glorify the now seen star through their future union and alliance. **It is the visible star that will become even more apparent!**

As previously mentioned, white dwarfs are stars like the sun in their dying age, and considering that more than 90 per cent of stars in the Milky Way are not actually like our sun, the odds of finding two sun-like stars to merge into one new star are very unlikely.

For centuries, the Church of Jesus has proclaimed the message of the Holy Trinity to the world. Some wholly believe, some partly believe and some don't. But if we examine this recent exposition and event objectively, it is evident that it precisely illuminates the biblical narrative of

Jesus' death, resurrection and union with the Holy Spirit as the Holy Ghost.

Also, considering that these recently discovered white dwarfs are both sun-like stars and our present sun is a celestial symbol for the Father pre-eminently exemplifies a mathematical precision of harmony. This epic event is a masterpiece and a grand gesture from above that shows that the concept of the Holy Trinity is indeed a revelation that's transcendent of our human reasoning.

MERCURY AND VENUS

According to astronomy, Mercury and Venus are terrestrial like the planet earth. In fact, certain astronomers have speculated that humans could someday live on Venus. However, life began on earth, which suggests that God deliberately chose earth for the emergence of life when he could have chosen Mercury or Venus.

Furthermore, Mercury and Venus have no moons whatsoever but the third planet with the first moon in our solar system is where life emerged (Selah).

Jesus said of himself in Revelation 1:8: *'I am Alpha and Omega, the beginning and the end, saith the lord, which is, and which was, and which is to come, the Almighty.'* As previously shown in the chapter on the moon, the earth's moon is an extra-terrestrial symbol of Jesus and the only known moon to orbit planet earth in our planetary system. Other planets have no moons or more than one moon but earth has only one.

Also, our solar system consists of several dwarf planets, which are not considered as planets in astronomy. But if we were to add these dwarf planets - Ceres, Pluto, Haumea, Makemake and Eris, as part of our solar system planets, it is the 'last' of the five dwarf planets - Eris, that happens to have 'one' moon as well – Selah.

There is only one true number that exists and that number is three. Three is the reason for every other number there is, and the first number to exist. **<u>Three is actually one</u>**! Life began at three and not one, just as we find with planet earth's pivotal position to the solar (sun) in the solar system.

MARS

The planet Mars, which is a neighbour to our planet, has been described by astronomers as a planet with an earth-like history. Planet scientists have found clear evidence of erosion on many surfaces on Mars that's reminiscent of large floods and small river systems. They speculate that at some time in Mars' past there must have been some liquid fluid on its surface, which suggests that the planet Mars may have sustained life forms as we have on earth today. Some astronomers even speculate that life on earth must have originated from Mars, and proposed that if the prehistoric waters on Mars can be found, it may lead to acquiring more substantial information about our cosmic beginning. 2 Peter 3:5–6 unveils a similar narrative, suggesting that a world existed before our world and that this world was flooded and destroyed by water.

Additionally, Mars has been confirmed to have two moons, while earth has only one moon that provides its stability. Conversely to earth's moon, Mars' two moons have proven inadequate to stabilise it. In the astronomical history of Mars, astronomers speculate that its moons were captured objects that strayed too close to Mars and were ensnared by its gravity, which implies that Mars' moons were not formed in the same way as earths'. Secular theories of astronomers maintain that the earth's moon experienced a unique birth formation, and is a child of the earth. However, Mars' moons are believed to be fully grown bodies of mass that were independently formed and later joined to sustain and manage Mars.

In a similar story to the forensic astronomy of Mars' moons, God created a fully grown man and woman (Adam and Eve) on the sixth day to 'subdue' and 'replenish' the earth (Genesis 1:28). To "subdue" and "replenish" suggests that there may have been previous losses suffered in the pre-Adamic world and that oppositions still existed in the earth, which could threaten the new order of creation. Despite God's forewarning, Adam and Eve failed in their assignment to exercise dominion over the 'intermediate stage' of the second earth and Adamic beginning, just as Mars' two moons failed to govern and manage Mars.

Further, like Mars' two adult moons history, Adam and Eve were created and made in adult form. Also, like the earth's moon child-like history, the lord Jesus came to earth in the form of a child.

In 1st Corinthians 15:45, Jesus is referred to as the 'last Adam', meaning that he shares a similar role and function as the first Adam and came to restore man to the original relationship man once had with God. In addition, 'Adam', meaning '<u>Earth</u>' and '<u>Man</u>', also means **'to be red'** in Hebrew. Incidentally, the last meaning of Adam's name ('red') coincides with astronomers' depiction of Mars as the red planet. And Earth, which is described in astronomy as the blue planet, coincides with the first meanings of Adam's name ('earth' and 'man'). It follows then, that Mars and its moons subtly encapsulate the symbolic affiliation between the first and second earth and their conflicting association with the conceptual story of Adam and Eve.

Astronomers have also confirmed that the position and motion of Mars' moons appear to be very different from that of our moon. The first moon of Mars, named Phobos, rises in the west and sets in the east, while its second moon, Deimos, rises in the east and sets in the west. Phobos' rise and fall is completed within 11 hours, while Deimos, using 30 hours for each orbit, takes 2.7 days to set in the west as it slowly falls behind the rotation of Mars to rise again. Phobos is a bit larger than Deimos and its orbit is below the synchronous altitude – consequently, the tidal forces lower its orbit. However,

Deimos orbits outside the synchronous altitude. Planet scientists fear that Phobos orbits too close to Mars and have predicted that in the near future, Phobos could crash into Mars' surface and break up into a ring structure surrounding Mars. It is said that no known moon orbits closer to its planet than Phobos, and as Phobos is gradually spiralling inward above the Martian surface, it draws about 1.8 metres closer to Mars each century, while Deimos continues to occupy a distant orbit across the surface of Mars.

If we compare the individual characteristics of Mars' two moons to the unique differences in males and females both now and in times past, the allegoric harmony between these two moons and the sexes of humanity is somewhat compatible. God made Adam before making Eve, as such; Adam appears to be closer to God than Eve. Adam is also given the power of position because of his first introduction to God.

As we observe from their story in Genesis 2 and 3, Adam was a covering over Eve, just as Phobos is a little larger than Deimos and orbits much closer to the surface of Mars than Deimos. Though Eve was the first to disobey God, according to Genesis, nothing significant transpired until Adam participated in this disobedient act because he was her spiritual covering. In fact, God frequently addressed them both as

Adam (Genesis 5:2), and it wasn't until after their disobedience and fall that Adam gave his wife the name Eve (Genesis 3:13–20). The unique difference in the astronomic story of Phobos and Deimos bring to mind a story as old as time – the battle of the sexes – the Garden of Eden, Eve and Adam, girls and boys, woman and man, ladies and gentlemen!

JUPITER AND THE

OTHER JOVIAN PLANETS

Jupiter is the first of the four outer planets. Planets after Jupiter are collectively known as the Jovian planets, namely Saturn, Uranus and Neptune. The Jovian planets (including Jupiter) collectively make up 99 per cent of the masses known to orbit the sun. However, these planets are not superior to the inner planets like Mercury, Venus, earth and Mars but are significantly different in composition.

Jupiter has been confirmed by astronomers as being eleven times the size of planet earth and is considered to be the biggest threat to the gravitational constant of our planet. Many astronomers refer to Jupiter as 'a failed star' because of its enormous size. It is often said by space astronomers that if Jupiter had been 80 times larger, it would have been a star and not a planet. Surprisingly, this astronomic view of Jupiter correlates with the Biblical view of angel Lucifer in Isaiah 14:12–14.

'How art thou fallen from heaven, O __Lucifer, son of the morning__! How art thou cut down to the ground, which didst weaken the nations! For thou hast said in thine heart, I will ascend into heaven, I will exalt my throne above the stars of God: I will sit also upon the mount of the congregation, in the sides of the north: I will ascend above the heights of the clouds; I will be like the Most High.'

Lucifer actually means 'bearer of light' and is also associated in meaning with stars. Conjointly, as the astronomic depiction of Jupiter is compared to a failed star, Lucifer is also a fallen angel. Astronomers have confirmed that Jupiter has a similar composition to that of our sun, and mainly consists of hydrogen and helium, which suggests that Jupiter aspires to emulate the sun, just like Lucifer's ambition to be as God.

Also correlatively, the name 'Jupiter' means Day Father. It is admittedly an Indo-European name that shows up in Sanskrit as *Dyaus-pita* and in Greek as *Zeus Jupiter*. It is also believed that the ancient Romans were the first to name Jupiter and had named the planet after their Roman god. In Roman mythology, Jupiter (or Jove) was depicted as the god of sky and thunder and was also regarded as the king of the gods.

'Day-Father' as the name implies suggests that that he who had come from 'day' (**Lucifer, the son of morning**) seeks to be equal with the Father (who is represented by the sun). As the sun is the parent star of our planetary system and lies at the heart of our solar system, providing life and light to planet earth, it appears Jupiter yearns to acquire the same position as the sun.

Additionally, the name 'Jupiter' and 'Lucifer' are syllabically related: Ju-Pi-Ter/Lu-Ci-Fer. But could the Romans have intentionally given this planet the name Jupiter to represent Lucifer? It is possible but unlikely. However, the scripture states the following in Proverb 20:24 *'Man's goings are of the lord; how can a man then understand his own way?'* – Selah.

Jupiter is also known to have an internal source of energy. Space astronomers have validated that Jupiter radiates twice as much energy as it receives from the sun. Some speculate that Jupiter's internal source of heat is due to the heat that is trapped inside the planet since its formation, which is now slowly leaking out. Others think that the planet is still contracting and expanding, and the gravitational energy from its orbiting natural satellites (i.e. moons) is converting into heat. A third speculation is that Jupiter, as opposed to an inside planet like earth does not have a crust and mantle of solid rocks, but is made of liquid hydrogen. And the convective motion in the liquid hydrogen of Jupiter enables it to emit heat more easily than the flow of heat through rocky matter and components of a planet like ours. It has also been confirmed by astronomers that Jupiter contains a complex and violent weather pattern, which includes extreme volcanic activity, huge storms and gigantic hurricanes.

Jupiter is also confirmed to have 63 known moons. Its internal source of heat, away from the sun, is partly due to the gravitational compression of its many surrounding moons and correlates with the biblical account of Lucifer and the pre-adamite nations he had corrupted and deceived to rebel against God (Isaiah 14:12). Also, Jupiter's orbit around the sun is indifferent to the other Jovian planets because it resembles a star in composition. Many planet scientists speculate that its process of formation (to become star-like) is still ongoing, though it resides within the solar system of our sun.

Furthermore, Jupiter marks the beginning of the outer planets in astronomy, which is similar to how Lucifer led the rebellion against God. The book of Revelations 12:3-4a paints a vivid allegoric narrative of how Lucifer deceived the other angels of heaven and brought them down to ruin as he did to himself. *'And there appeared another wonder in heaven; **a great red dragon**, seven heads and ten horns, and seven crowns upon his heads. **And his*** *tail drew the third part of the stars of heaven, and did cast them to earth...'* Though, the scriptures do not reveal how many angels were deceived by Lucifer, it states that a third part of the stars of heaven were cast down to earth.

Surprisingly, planet Jupiter has three other planets like it (previously mentioned). All four planets, including Jupiter constitute the Jovian planets. Also, Jupiter's predominant weather pattern, known as 'the great red spot' in astronomy complements the biblical depiction of Lucifer as 'the great red dragon' (Revelations 12:3).

And despite planet Jupiter's similar composition to the sun – hydrogen and helium, it has been confirmed to contain most of the non-plasma in our solar system (plasma is water in a different state and form). This suggests that Jupiter has no true relation to the sun and the entire solar system. Usually, there is plasma in the sun and the stars, even the space between planets and stars is filled with sparse quantities of plasma. But like the biblical story of Lucifer, planet Jupiter is an outsider and a stranger.

Additionally, Jupiter, like Lucifer who fell from grace, is the only Jovian planet viewed by astronomers as a failed star and is still characterised by its ambition to become a star. Also,

Jupiter along with Saturn, Uranus and Neptune appear to form a miniature solar system of their own because of their many orbiting moons as they circle the sun. Evidently, a rebellious streak is ingrained in their behavioural pattern. While Jupiter has 63 known moons, Saturn has 62, Uranus has 32 and Neptune has 18. All four Jovian planets in astronomy are also named the 'outside planets'. In Revelation 12:9, the scripture confirms *'And the great dragon was **cast out**, that old serpent, called the Devil, and Satan, which deceiveth the whole world: he was **cast out** into the earth, and his angels were **cast out** with him.'*

Saturn, the second planet in the Jovian category, is bland in exterior and distinguished by its extensive ring system. However, a disturbing complexity lies beneath its attractive surface. The old adage 'The devil is in the details' sums up the astronomic narrative of Saturn. Unlike Jupiter, Uranus and Neptune, which are known to have very dark rings, Saturn's rings are magnificently attractive, pretty and bright. When astronomers look at Saturn through an optical telescope, they often see its day side and a sunlit view of its rings. However, with the Cassini voyage in recent years, astronomers have acquired startling information about Saturn's internal structure. They have collected data to make measurements that are possible through visits to Saturn, and recently confirmed that

Saturn also has a night side. Astronomers observed tiny storms that even powerful telescopes were not able to see in times past. A certain Dr Linda Spilker, who was the deputy project scientist for the Cassini–Huygens mission, confirmed that the new information provided new perspectives on Saturn's atmosphere and internal structure. The Cassini mission revealed many surprising similarities between Saturn's internal structure and Jupiter's. For example, the poles of Saturn possess monstrous whirling mass of air and heat that generates giant thunderstorms. Who would have guessed that the beautiful-looking Saturn had such strong vortexes underneath its surface?

Similarly, 2nd Corinthians 4:4 states that Satan, who is the god of this world (systems), has blinded the minds of those who do not believe. It is one of his many amazing talents. 2nd Corinthians 11:13–14 also sheds more light about this chameleonic gift of Satan: *'For such are false apostles, deceitful workers, transforming themselves into the apostles of Christ. And no marvel; for* **Satan himself is transformed into an angel of light** [which means Satan can sometimes disguise himself to be an angel of heaven, e.g. archangel Michael or Gabriel].'

Satan is the second identity of Lucifer and please note that this verse of scripture refers to him as 'Satan', and not 'Lucifer', the

'Devil' or 'the accuser of the brethren'. Surprisingly, Saturn (like Jupiter and Lucifer) also shares a similar biblical paradigm in oral and name syllables, Sa-Turn/Sa-Tan. Sa-'Turn' here suggests a turn around, a transformation of his countenance, just as the aforementioned scripture highlighted. Though it is unusual for planets to twinkle, however, planet Saturn twinkles at times – allegedly because of its turbulent atmosphere and its even-coloured bland exterior. This odd aberration typifies the biblical account of Satan as a disguised star and angel of light.

Saturn, like Jupiter, has also been confirmed to have its own internal source of energy and also radiates twice as much energy as it receives from the sun. A significant difference between Saturn and Jupiter is that Jupiter is associated with expansion while Saturn is associated with contraction. As relating to expansion, Lucifer still seeks to establish his kingdom in heaven and hopes to influence more angels belonging to heaven. As relating to contraction, Satan has already established his kingdom here on earth and is looking to incarcerate new earthly recruits. Also, as Jupiter is before Saturn in astronomy, Lucifer is also before Satan in the scriptures. And both Jupiter and Saturn are paired in astronomy, alternatively known as the gas giants.

Uranus, the third planet in the Jovian category, is the lightest of the outer planets in body mass, and it has a much cooler core than Jupiter and Saturn and is often described by scientist as an ice giant. Due to Uranus' distance from the sun, its chemical compounds freeze at a much lower temperature than the planets closer to the sun. The sunlight we receive here on earth would seem like twilight in Uranus' region. So naturally, Uranus has no internal source of heat and cannot radiate as much energy as Jupiter or Saturn.

However, Neptune, another ice giant and the fourth planet in the Jovian category, is further from the sun than Uranus but behaves like Jupiter and Saturn. Though Neptune possesses fewer moons than Uranus, which means it is less likely to convert gravitational energy into heat, yet astronomers have found that it radiates twice as much energy, just like Jupiter and Saturn. Neptune is not nearly as hot as Jupiter and Saturn because of its reduced size and mass and its location in a colder region than Uranus. So its ability to burn at a high temperature and radiate more energy than it draws from the sun is a strange phenomenon. Neptune and Uranus are often described as twins because of their composition of ice; though, Neptune, which should be colder than Uranus still manages to own its internal source of heat. The odd contrast between Uranus and

Neptune suggests that the Jovian planets' ability to generate heat and have a different source of energy away from the sun borders on the mysterious. Evidently, the unique characteristics of each Jovian planet convey a deeper meaning than human science can fathom. It is evident that these planets exist to confirm biblical narratives.

Furthermore, the Father, the Son, Lucifer and his angels, like the sun, moon and the four Jovian planets, are the only celestial objects in our solar system with halo rings! While the sun and the moon's halo ring are considered to be formed by tiny ice crystals that have been gathered as cirrus or wispy clouds bent and diffracted by sunlight, the Jovian planet rings are formed by the breakup of other satellite bodies. Though Jovian planets rings may contain ice crystals like the sun and moon, but they also contain rock and sand particles, which is suggestive of a violent acquisition of power!

Lastly, it has been confirmed by astronomers that the asteroid belt mainly occupies the orbit between Mars (symbolic of the first earth and the condemned pre-Adamite race) and Jupiter (symbolic of Lucifer and his fallen angels). Astronomers speculate that these asteroids are remainders from the solar system's formation process, which failed to coalesce due to the gravitational interference of Jupiter. And that Jupiter's longing to pull and control the earth has been a major concern in astronomy to date. However, it is and has always been the earth's moon (symbolic of Jesus) that prevents the gravitational pull of Jupiter from tilting and toppling the earth over to its ferocious demands.

ALIENS

Till date, the Search for Extra-terrestrial Intelligence Institute (SETI), established in the late 1950s, has not found anything conclusive on alien higher life forms. Aliens have never been seen entering into our atmosphere from outside planet earth. However, there is the hypothesis that aliens visit earth in physical spacecrafts (i.e. UFOs – which we shall address later) and another inter-dimensional hypothesis that suggests aliens visit earth from other dimensions. Contrary to secular reasoning, the latter hypothesis lends itself to a spiritual and religious appeal, and if we choose to believe the latter, we are no longer speaking of a scientific subject but a spiritual matter.

The basis for the former hypothesis is evolution: the idea that life here on earth is accidental and may have occurred elsewhere, which is still not substantiated. The earth cannot be accidental if it reflects intelligent and creative design. For example, the planet earth is the *third* planet from the sun; the liquid water that sustains life forms on earth and is mandatory for any potential life forms on another planet is also *three* in composition. It consists of two hydrogen gas molecules and one oxygen gas molecule. An atom, which is considered to be the building block of all matter (i.e. anything material or physical), is also *tripartite*, consisting of electron, proton and neutron. And sub-atoms, which make up atoms, also have *tripartite* sub-divisions. Sub-atomic protons contain two up quarks and one down quark, and neutrons contain one up quark and two down quarks. Space is height, depth and width. Time is past, present and future. All these clues point to the doctrine of the triune deity, as the scriptures predict in Romans 1:20.

If there are any aliens for humans to see, the scriptures propose that such aliens are not 'extra solar planet creatures' but spiritual beings. Synchronically, this is what our best efforts have demonstrated. What we find continues to elude us and these findings have already been exposed in the scriptures. 'Biblical aliens' are mentioned through the pages of the Bible and are depicted as celestial beings who take on terrestrial forms. In the last chapter of Hebrews 13:2, the apostle Paul informs the church brethren: *'Be not forgetful to entertain strangers: for thereby some have entertained angels unawares.'*

The scriptures explicitly record that angels and the lord Jesus have often visited humans in times past. Genesis 18:1–2 is an example: *'And the Lord appeared to him* [Abraham] *in the plains of Mamre: and he sat in the tent door in the heat of the day: And he lifted up his eyes and looked, and, lo three men stood by him: and when he saw them, he ran to meet them from the tent door, and bowed himself toward the ground.'*

Genesis 19:1: *'And there came two angels to Sodom at even; and Lot sat in the gate of Sodom: and Lot seeing them rose up to meet them; and he bowed himself with his face toward the ground.'* Also, Luke 1:28 adds: *'And the angel came to her, and said, Hail, thou that art highly favoured, the Lord is with thee: blessed art thou among women, And when she saw him, she was troubled at his saying, and cast in her mind what manner of salutation this should be.'*

In modern history, one widely-known example of celestial visitations was in the case of Prophet William Branham. In a picture of him in the Sam Houston Coliseum on the night of January 24th, 1950, an apparent halo of light was seen above his head. William Branham had previously acknowledged the presence of an angel standing two feet from where he stood and had often mentioned this in his church services. A copy of this verified picture is held in the Library of Congress in Washington, D.C.

In past and recent times, fossils of 'prehistoric' skulls and bones have been unearthed by archaeologists. Historic humans have also been unearthed and are categorised as Homo-sapiens (i.e. you and I). Conjointly, scientists have assigned similar terms for findings of other homo species fossils. Examples of such terms are the Homo-erectus, who allegedly arrived in Flores in the Middle Pleistocene sometime between 781,000 and 126,000 years ago. Other examples are the Homo-floresiensis, Homo-habilis, Homo-georgicus and Homo-neanderthalensis. All these archaic homos were identified from fossils. And it is from these findings that theories of evolution have surmised.

Often times, secular scientists assume that the Biblical God (if real) is unaware of prehistoric times, and that they have cleverly found him out to be false. However, the scriptures clearly express that God intended for prehistoric evidences to be found. It was God who first penned the words of the Torah on two tables of stone with Moses at Mount Sinai (Exodus 32:15–16), and a second time, instructed Moses to write in like manner (Exodus 34:27–29). It was God who told Moses past and future events so that Moses could record historical accounts of ancient family genealogies, the story of creation and many other unique stories of men who lived before (and even after) Moses. God has always been a writer and an historian. In Exodus 17:14, it is written: *'And the Lord said unto Moses, write this for a memorial in a book, and rehearse it in the ears of Joshua…'*

God could have obliterated the pre-Adamic earth with fire, but didn't. He could have destroyed the second earth in the days of Noah with fire, but didn't. Instead he destroyed both worlds with water so we could later find evidences for prehistoric and historical life as recorded in scriptures. God is a story teller and the best there is. It's no wonder the Bible is still the bestselling book of all time.

Prophet Jeremiah confirmed the existence of prehistoric times when he published his prophetic travel in a space 'between times' (i.e. the pre-Adamic world and the present Adamic world) in Jeremiah 4:23–28: *'I beheld the earth and lo, it was without form and void; and the heavens, and they had no light* [Genesis 1:2]. *I beheld the mountains, and, lo, they trembled, and all the hills moved lightly. I beheld, and, lo, there was no man, and all the birds of the heavens were fled* [that is to say, there were previous inhabitants in the earth of men and birds before the story in Genesis 1:2 began]. *I beheld, and, lo, the fruitful place was a wilderness, and all the cities thereof were broken down at the presence of the LORD, and by his fierce anger* [elaborated in 2 Peter 3:6–7]. *For thus hath the LORD said, the whole land shall be* *desolate; **yet will I not make a full end** [meaning that God 'purposely intended' to leave an evidence of the prehistoric era]. For this shall the earth mourn, and the heavens above be black: because I have spoken it, I have purposed it, and will not repent, neither will I turn back from it.'*

Additionally, prophet Isaiah, in his prophetic travel to prehistoric times also confirmed that there were nations of people living during the days of Lucifer. Isaiah 14:12 narrates: *'How art thou fallen from heaven, O Lucifer, son of the morning! How art thou cut down to the ground, **who weakened the nations?'***

Prophet Ezekiel also wrote of a much older prehistoric time when Lucifer previously walked in the first Garden of Eden (Ezekiel 28:13). In a narrative revealing God's reserved judgement for the anticipated antichrist (the prince of Tyrus – Ezekiel 28:1–10), the prehistoric flood and creation were mentioned. Ezekiel 28:7–8: *'Behold, therefore I [God speaking] will bring **strangers** upon thee, **the terrible of the nations**: and they shall draw their swords against the beauty of thy wisdom, and they shall defile thy brightness. **They shall bring thee down to the pit and thou shall die the deaths of them that are slain in the midst of the seas.'***

These prehistoric beings, according to the scriptures, were the pre-Adamite race who suffered God's judgement in the flooding of the world before ours (2 Peter 3:7–8). They were the residents in the pits of hell who spoke to Lucifer after he fell from grace (Isaiah 14:15–16); they are the demons and unclean spirits that roam the face of the earth today (Isaiah 24:1). Their bones and skulls are some of the unique fossil findings many archaeologists keep and store in their laboratories.

In addition, there have also been fossils unearthed from the flood in the days of Noah. However, the focus of our topic here is astronomy and not archaeology, so please pardon my diversion; I intend to return to astronomy through the alleys of archaeology. It is necessary to include archaeology in the subject of aliens because demonic spirits are the previous terrestrial inhabitants of our planet and need to be differentiated from the angelic celestial inhabitants of planet earth in times past.

The pre-adamic creations (now known as demons) are disembodied spirits and no longer own material bodies that are visible in the earthly realm since their death in the pre-adamic flood.

However, they may appear to have bodies if God allows us to see into the supernatural or if demons invoke visions and hallucinations of themselves in the mind of their victims. Though demons can often move objects and inflict physical harm, since their death, they remain bodiless in the earth realm. This is the primary reason they often house themselves in the bodies of humans or animals to cohabitate on earth.

Where we find confrontations between humans and demons in biblical narratives, demons are not portrayed as having a visible body but are often communicated with, through the possessed body of a human or an animal (e.g. Matthew 8:28-33).

Angels, however, whether heavenly or fallen, were originally created with celestial bodies and are capable of exhibiting inter-dimensional polymorphism. Their bodies can alter their shape and form, materialise and dematerialise in the earthly dimension. Even after the fall of Lucifer and his angels, they still kept their celestial bodies (Luke 20:36). The scripture identifies both the celestial and terrestrial types of bodies in 1 Corinthians 15:39-40, and in Colossians 1:16, the scripture records that both the celestial and terrestrial were created by our Lord Jesus. It is shown in the Bible that both angels and demons predate humanity and if either is seen by us, they would be regarded as aliens.

However, beside angels and demons, which are often depicted in the Bible as having different odd forms and shapes, are the cruel jokes of numerous alien hoaxes. Many of these jesters propagate horrific news that misinforms the public. And even the much feared anticipation of aliens invading our planet has already transpired in primitive times and is recorded in the Bible (Genesis 6:1-9). The book of Jude 1:6-7 reflects on this aberrational event - *And the angels which kept not their first estate, but left their own habitation, he [God] hath reserved in everlasting chains under darkness unto the judgment of the great day. Even as Sodom and Gomorrah, and the cities about them in like manner, giving themselves over to fornication, and going after strange flesh, are set forth for an example, suffering the vengeance of eternal fire.*

These fallen angels, described by Jude as the 'strange flesh' that fornicated with humans in the days of Noah, were celestial rebels and outlaws who left their divinely ordained boundaries in the cosmos (will come back to this) to cohabitate with humans on earth. These angels most probably possessed humanoid bodies, which fits the description of certain angels in the Bible (e.g. angel Gabriel in Daniel 9:21). For their unruly defiance and misconduct, they received a judicial verdict of eternal justice and punishment from God and are till this day, imprisoned in the underworld. Their story is similar to the imprisoned criminals here on earth who sit on death row, awaiting a final termination. Beside them, are other fallen angels who did not trespass their divinely ordained boundaries "in the days of Noah". These remaining fallen angels, including the fallen Lucifer, are among the angelic host who sometimes visit earth and disguise themselves as cosmic aliens and enlightened beings (2 Corinthians 11:14-15).

In later years, after the floods of Noah, the inhabitants of the earth ambitiously desired to transcend their earthly boundary and make a name for themselves like the fallen Lucifer (Isaiah 14:12-15). Unbeknownst to them, their prideful ambition had a potential to restore the former union that fallen angels had with humans. They had hoped to erect a tower that could reach the heavens - midway between the cosmos and the earth, and this tower would have served as a sort of ladder to bridge the gap between the terrestrial earth and the celestial heaven.

The problem with this is that God beforehand had punished the fallen angelic hosts, particularly those who exceeded their ordained boundaries in the cosmos and descended to earth to cohabitate with humans (Jude 1:6-7). Now, the generations after Noah - chiefly motivated by pride, were blindly pursuing a potential relationship with the celestial sphere (again!). Our current S.E.T.I establishment (search for extra-terrestrial intelligence) somewhat resembles the remote antiquity of the people of the Babylonian tower. As far back as this story is and as odd as it may seem, the contemporary ambition of SETI institute, and several like-minded organisations, are pursuing a similar goal by trying to communicate with the celestial heavens or associate with it solely through physical and non-spiritual means. (See Genesis 11:4-6 for the narratives of the tower of Babel and Genesis 6:2-5)

Historically, humans who emerged since the fall of Adam until the day that Jesus was resurrected, were the first to assume celestial beings had originated from the cosmos. It seemed natural for many of them to believe this lie that satan and the fallen angels had concocted. Since the fallen angels no longer belonged to the third heaven and previously had the ambition to dethrone God, they devised a deceitful scheme to appear as deity gods who had come from the third heaven to lord over humans. Though, in actual reality, they were fallen angels who had acquired influence between the third heaven and earth due to Adam's fall (Job 1:6-7). This new privilege enabled satan and his angels to create a vague resemblance of what he envisioned in time past, which was to impersonate God (Isaiah 14:14).

satan's new status and privilege was enforced by an established command from God to Adam and Eve not to eat from the forbidden tree, which Adam and Eve's disobedient actions legislated. This enacted law is identified in the scriptures as the law of sin and death (Romans 8:2c) and it is on this legal ground that the fallen Lucifer rose to power again as satan.

It was feasible for satan to create this pseudo-deity image for himself and his bandit of angels, and to deceive the inhabitants of planet earth especially as he was now capable of influencing the cosmic heavens. However, just as the astronomer who travels to the moon cannot be 'a cosmic alien' because he does not originate from the moon. The same is true for angelic creatures, whether heavenly or fallen. They are not cosmic aliens. Their descent is either heaven or hades, and as the Bible reveals: fallen angels are creatures that originally fell from the third heaven and are ultimately bound to the depths of the underworld.

The acquisition of satan's temporary power over the second heavens is one of the chief reasons behind the Roman and Greek mythological beliefs in astronomical gods (Acts 19:35). Fictional theories like extra-solar aliens were cleverly concocted by evil forces to weaken and undermine the authority of the scriptures, and to introduce an alternative view for our cosmic origin.

satan's primary purpose since the creation of mankind is to make us disbelieve the words of God. His first words to Eve in Eden were: **_Yea, hath God said_**, *Ye shall not eat every tree of the garden?* (Genesis 3:1). Since his fall as Lucifer and the creation of the world of Adam and Eve, satan works very hard to discredit God among God's new creation. A belief in unbiblical aliens will certainly contribute to his deceitful sophistry. It can change the way the world views itself and has done so for many of us.

Surprisingly, many of those who assent to believe in secular theories of aliens' higher life forms have never themselves encountered an alien or seen one before. Colossians 2:18 admonishes - *Let no man beguile* [deceive] *you of your* [heavenly] *reward in a voluntary humility* [participation] *and worshipping of angels* [i.e. obsessing and adoring of angels], *intruding into those things which he hath not seen, vainly puffed up by his fleshy mind.* Needless to say, the scriptures does not deny the existence of angels but warns here that angelic beings are not to be adored or made into idols and objects of worship by men.

There are several verses in the Bible that eliminate a plausible notion of faith in aliens' higher life forms. For example, Hebrews 2:5–9 states:

'For unto the angels hath he [God] **not** *put in subjection* [i.e. in control of] *the world to come, whereof we speak. But one in a certain place testified saying, what is man that thou art mindful of him? Or the son of man, that thou visits him? Thou made him a little lower than the angels; thou crowned him with glory and honour, and did set him over the works of thy hands: Thou hast put* <u>**all**</u> [all means ALL] *things in subjection under his feet* [i.e. in his control]. *For in that he* [God] *put all in subjection under him* [humans], *he* [God] *left nothing that is not put under him* [suggests that there could be no other possible higher beings elsewhere, like 'unbiblical aliens' except for angels]. *But we see not yet all things put under him* [meaning it doesn't seem like this is so]. *But* [when] *we see Jesus* [who was] *made a little lower than the angels for the suffering of death, crowned with glory and honour; that he* [Jesus] *by the grace of God should taste death for every man* [meaning Jesus' death at the cross could restore the original intent of God for humanity. So therefore, every man and woman has the potential to live an extraordinary life like Jesus].'

Another biblical insight that eliminates a plausible notion of belief in cosmic aliens is concealed in Genesis 1:16: *'And God made two great lights; the greater light* [sun] *to rule the day and the lesser light* [moon] *to rule the night: he made the stars also.'* It may seem absurd that God deliberately mentioned the sun and moon before acknowledging five hundred billion stars but there is a reason for this as we will soon find. There are certain questions that one may ask if we examine this verse closely:

i.   **Is the Biblical God aware that the sun is also one of the five hundred billion stars in the cosmos?**

He certainly is. In Psalm 8:3, as David worshipped God in the Spirit, he described the heavens from the perspective of a secular astronomer: *'When I consider Your heavens, the work of Your fingers, <u>the moon and the stars</u>, which You have ordained'* Notice that the scriptures did not differentiate the sun from the stars in this verse. Evidently, it was accepted that the sun was a star as well. However, in Psalms 136:7–9, the same David in the Spirit of worship distinguished the sun from the stars by appropriating the celestial lights in the order established by God in Genesis. *'To him that made great lights: for his mercy endureth forever:* **the sun to rule by day**: *for his mercy endureth forever:* **the moon and stars to rule by night**: *for his mercy endureth forever.'*

In addition, the book of Job 38:31–33 recites the names of the celestial stars, which indicates that the biblical God is intricately mature in his knowledge of the cosmic stars and space: *'Canst thou bind the sweet influences of Pleiades, or loose the bands of Orion? Canst thou bring forth Mazzaroth in his season? Or canst thou guide Arcturus with his sons? Knowest thou the ordinances of heaven: canst thou set the dominion thereof in the earth?'* In Psalms 147:4, it is written: *'He [God] telleth the number of the stars; he calleth them all by their names.'* Evidently, God is aware that the sun is a star but chooses to distinguish it from other stars. So why is this (one may ask)?

ii. **Why is the sun portrayed as a stronger character in comparison to five hundred billion stars in the galaxies, and what makes the sun so unique?**

As illustrated in previous pages of this volume, the sun is a celestial symbol for the Father, and because of the Father's executive position in the divine trinity, the sun is also given the privilege of position among other stars. What makes our sun so unique in comparison to every star, including stars like our sun is probably not its astrophysical composition, its size or age; There is a high probability of finding a sun-like star with a similar history and future like our sun. However, the

141

difference between our sun and other sun-like stars has always been **EARTH**! <u>**We are the difference!!**</u>

If we believe in theories of unbiblical aliens, this would suggest that we believe in more than one sun and also believe in more than one Heavenly Father. The scripture is clear in pointing out that only one sun exists! If the Bible had suggested two or more suns, then theories of unbiblical aliens would have been scripturally valid. Two or more suns from the scriptures would suggest that God indeed created other beings living in the extra-solar planets – like we live here on earth. But the Bible intentionally omits this! God would never have distinguished the sun from the stars in the scriptures if there was the slightest possibility of living beings in other planetary systems. The purpose of the one sun is to serve as the celestial symbol for the Father God. And the sun, moon and stars were primarily made as signs for the Holy Trinity (Genesis 1:14b).

In real astronomic science, there is no feasible evidence to support the view that humans have been in contact with aliens that originate from solar or extra solar planets. This is because no human has physically travelled to anywhere in space but the moon.

Furthermore, space scientists have not identified any solar or extra-solar planet that's known to be occupied by aliens.

Also, UFO – **Unidentifiable** Flying Object, as the acronym means implies that secular theorists do not really know what it is. Notwithstanding, it is true that UFOs (Unidentifiable Flying Objects) have been seen on radar by many credible witnesses, and are often described as travelling lights in the sky or flying disks that resemble a spacecraft.

These occasional anomalies in the skies are often demonic manifestations contrived by fallen angels to create misguided beliefs in the existence of cosmic aliens and spread fallacious ideas that would appeal to modern science and human society. By materialising what resembles a modern spacecraft in the skies (the first heaven), it would seem like cosmic aliens may indeed exist in other solar planets. However, there has been no observed manifestation of this kind in the cosmos (the second heavens) in recent centuries, and we shall find the biblical reason for this as we continue reading.

The scriptures often describe satan and his angels as masters of deceits and disguise because this is what they do best. Several victims of 'alien abduction' view their abductors as spiritual and enlightened beings, which evidently sound like the biblical admonishment and warnings of humans encountering fallen angels. (Galatians 1:8, 2 Corinthians 11:14). Unsurprisingly, some of these abductors often make odious or erroneous remarks about Jesus and the Bible.

In other unique cases, UFOs can be angelic visitations from the third heaven. In the story leading to the birth of Jesus Christ, the scriptures record that there was a 'star' that led the wise men to Jesus in Bethlehem. But what was this star? Was it an ordinary celestial star or something we would call a UFO? Whatever it was, it is evident that this star had a miraculous origin. The gospel of Matthew records that this star *'went before them* [i.e. the wise men, travelling from east to west]*, till it came and stood over where the young Child was'* (Matthew 2:9). Ordinary stars are not capable of moving and changing directions. Even shooting stars cannot halt over a specific location. It is possible that this star was an angel (a Biblical alien). Angels are known to radiate a glorious appearance like stars and can move and change directions to lead a way.

In the days before the resurrection of Jesus, it was possible to observe demonic UFO's in the cosmic heavens. Acts 19:35 informs - *And when the townclerk had appeased the people, he said, Ye men of Ephesus,* **what man is there that knoweth not**

how that the city of the Ephesians is a worshipper of the great
goddess Diana, and of the image which fell down from Jupiter?

It is not surprising that this strange occurrence is associated
with the planet Jupiter. The chapter on Jupiter explains what
Jupiter represents. Though the town clerk had reported this
event like a recent happening in the days of the early church,
his confession betrayed the present and showed that this was a
past event!

Before the resurrection of Jesus from the dead, satan and his
fallen angels often obstructed the pathway of heavenly angels
during their travels (through the cosmos) to and fro the third
heaven. Examples in the scriptures are Archangel Michael on
his ascension to the third heaven (with the dead body of Moses
Jude 1:9) and Archangel Gabriel on his descent to earth (with
the answer to Daniel's prayers – Daniel 10:12-13). Until Jesus'
descent into hell and his resurrection from the dead
(Revelation 1:18), satan held the keys of hell and death and
this key ensphered the cosmic heavens. Infact, no departed
saints could ascend into heaven, except Moses! And this could
not have transpired without a confrontation between angel
Michael and the Devil (in my book - The Mystery, we shall
find the reason for Moses' ascension, we shall also discuss

145

Elijah's and Enoch's translations into heaven, the only three men who ascended to Heaven before Jesus' death and resurrection).

The scriptures record that the saints who departed before Jesus' death resided in father Abraham's bosom, which was located beside hades - Luke 16:22-23. The resurrection of the old saints and their ascension into the third heaven was the first miracle after Jesus' resurrection (Matthew 27:52-53). Jesus took from satan the keys of hell and death, so we can freely ascend into heaven after death.

Heavenly angels, which are also cosmic travellers, were at a disadvantage in fulfilling many of their assignments before Jesus' resurrection (Daniel 10:12-21). The role is now reversed: the fallen angels are the ones disadvantaged in this present age and time. However, these roles will be reversed again temporarily during the reign of the antichrist, who would rule in the earth for sometime (Revelation 12:6-8). The reason for this temporary transition is because what is permitted on earth will often reflect in the cosmic heavens (Psalm 115:16). Matthew 18:18 expounds: *'Verily I say unto you, Whatsoever you shall bind on earth shall be bound in heaven: and whatsoever ye shall loose on earth shall be loosed in heaven.'*

In correlation to the Garden of Eden, what man loosed on earth when he disobeyed God was also loosed in the heavens; this was how satan and the fallen angels gained access to the cosmic heavens after the fall of Adam and Eve.

Evil principalities and powers can still operate and manifest in the first heavens (i.e. the earth's sky) today because the primal law of sin and death still prevails in the children of disobedience (Ephesians 2:2b), especially in regions where the name of Jesus is unknown and despised (Romans 15:20, 22. 1 Thessalonians 2:14-18). However, they cannot traffic the second heavens any longer (except during the antichrist's rulership).

Jesus is the present new authority (Matthew 28:18) and his departed saints must be escorted by the angels in their ascension into heaven. After the reign of the antichrist on earth is done, the fallen angels' position in the heavens will be **permanently** removed. The victory over the evil principalities in the cosmic heavens will be accomplished a second time through the same death and resurrection of Jesus at Calvary (Revelation 12:11 calls this 'the blood and testimony').

Fallen angels who tell their human abductors that they are solar and extra-solar aliens, do so to undermine the integrity of the scriptures and to attack the testimony of the resurrection of

Christ, which displaced their position in the cosmic heavens. The law of the life of the spirit in Christ Jesus gives the redeemed on earth shelter from fallen angels – also known as evil principalities and powers (Romans 12:2) but these fallen principalities and powers can still oppress those who are under the previous law of sin and death.

Many of the things we associate with, and attribute to the unseen laws of the universe (e.g. "the law of attraction") are actualised by angelic (heavenly or fallen) and demonic forces, but some of us cannot tell what is what until much later. Those who have a relationship with God's word can discern the difference between what is good and the appearance of good (Hebrews 4:12). One can be easily deceived by demonic forces if their only focus is a desired end. Enquiring about the source and means of an outcome is a necessary prerequisite if we intend to walk in the light. There is an old African proverb that sheds light on the enticement of deception – *'Not all that glitters is gold'*.

A distinguished scientist by the name of Gary Bates proposed a universal question on the subject of Aliens. He asked: *'Why is the world so big?'* and brilliantly answered - *'Because God is!'*

satan prefers that we show unhealthy interest in the affairs of the cosmos, he wants the glory that belongs to God.

However, the heavens and the heaven is all about God's glory and nothing else (Psalm 19:1-4). The prayer of Jesus in Matthew 6:9 confirms this: '...*Our Father who art in Heaven, Hallowed be thy name*'.

VOLUME 1

'In spite of persuasive scientific evidence pointing to a genuine starting point for the universe – the famous 'big bang' – science is incapable of telling us why it happened or who or what 'happened' it. Nor can philosophical 'cosmological arguments' prove by what agency the universe was formed; at best they can argue in favour of a 'first cause'. …So where does this extra information come from? It comes to us by revelation or not at all.'

- Prof. Edgar H. Andrews

THE GENESIS CODE

'In the beginning, God created the heaven and the earth'

- Genesis 1:1

I heard this somewhere and it has stayed with me ever since – 'Every story has a beginning'. But imagine a story without a beginning, imagine a world without end – this is the story of God, unwritten before the books of Genesis and Revelation, before angels or humans, before anything was created or formed. It is a story older than time, before the stars and moon, before the sun and the universe, a story where 'unending' makes perfect sense because there was never a beginning to start with.

Imagine… imagine, imagine. Imagine a story without a history, imagine a reality that has always been and has never been without existence. No starting point! No pause or intervals, no full stops, without origin, beyond origin, pre-original. Imagine! You can't, can you? It's not your fault if you can't; we were born that way. 'WE' as soul and body (with the exception of a spirit) were created with a beginning so how can we think or feel any differently. This was my dilemma at the age of four and five as I lay back in open air during midnight hours, staring at the thick blanket of the stars and moon above until I fell asleep.

When I was a kid, I did not give God much rest at night and almost drove myself insane thinking the unthinkable. I had many questions of the same kind, obsessive and never-ending questions that made me stay up late at night. The mental challenge of resolving and reconciling the history of creation with the history of the God who created it is certainly overwhelming for any child to bear and understand but I never stopped searching for the answers to my questions – like who is God? Where did He come from? How was He born? How did He get started? Does He have parents? If He does, where did they come from? Did He have a little help? Did He just come out of nothing or was there a little bit of something already existing? Who put the little something there? Where did that come from? The air, the wind, fire, rocks, sand, water, sky and all vegetation - where did they all come from? What about me? How is it possible I can think or imagine? How is it possible I can speak and feel? Why am I asking these questions? How is it possible that I have these questions? How? Where? Why? How did it all begin? How could anything be? After a while I'd stop, and then continue, stop, and then continue. It was exhausting and tiring, it was pointless and unimaginative but I could not resist the obsession to start all over again: Who is God? Where did He come from? ...

I will be the first to admit it; I was a weird kid. But what kid isn't? I had more heart than brains, what else can I say? I was smart in a stupid way. I knew there were no possible answers to these questions but believed that someday, somehow, I would realise the infinite knowledge to uncover this mystery and decipher the Genesis code.

Before embarking on the journey of seeking God, it's important we consider that we cannot find what we have not yet defined. God means different things to different people. Several dictionaries and religions associate different definitions and meanings for God. However, the one conventional definition and notion associated with God is that God created everything there is (including you and I). This definition of God 'as a creator' is the principal subject for this volume.

In the human mind, everything that exists is expected to have a beginning. But considering that God is uncreated and without a beginning, the right questions to inquire of God should be: Who is God before creation, before the beginning of anything there is, before his identity and existence as a creator, who was God?

The solution to this conundrum will be the key to unlock the greatest conceivable revelation of God there is! It is the mystery that has engendered all other mysteries. To understand who God is, we have to look beyond and behind God as a creator to see if there is anything else. This and much more is what we shall find in the third volume.

For now, let us consider the following: If God isn't, we may ask who is God (?) but if God is, we need not ask who is God but who God is! The book of Hebrews 11:6 states the

155

following: *"But without faith it is impossible to please him: for he that cometh to God must believe that he is, and that he is a rewarder of them that diligently seek him"*.

There are two important things to note from this verse of scripture (and a third that's befitting):

- If indeed we are searching for God, we must first believe that God exists.
- And if we believe that God exists, we should also believe that God will reward us according to our demonstration of faith in him.
- Please note that this biblical verse was written on the premise that we choose the Christian faith.

As shown from the above, who and what we choose to believe, and how we exercise our faith is just as important as the revelation of God to us. We have a part to play if we must discover who God is. It follows therefore, that the question – who is God (?), is not the same as who God is (!), because the former is asked irresponsibly and doubtfully while the latter is asked through an exercise and demonstration of faith.

An answer is only as good as its question. If a question asked is vague and uncertain, so will the answer that follows but if a question asked is specific and certain, so will the answer that follows. The right answer is everywhere we look but we cannot see it if we do not ask the right questions. Ironically, there is no right answer 'for a wrong question' no matter where we look, and however hard we search.

In correlation to the paragraph above, the narratives of Genesis cannot suffice to reveal the entirety of God to us, because God existed before creation. So then, the book of Genesis cannot make an exhaustive biography for God because God himself is without a Genesis or beginning (God is continually revealed to us through a chosen medium of revelation). Howbeit, the narratives of Genesis may suffice to tell us of the works of creation and can also assist in uncovering the secret identity of the creator of our universe and existence.

THE THIRD DAY OF CREATION

(More on the Sun, Moon and Stars)

While writing the second volume of this book (which I wrote before the first volume), I heard the voice of God spoke to my heart that he had made the sun, the moon and the stars on the 3rd day of creation. I wanted to believe his voice but it was so difficult to accept this information because it was radically new to me and was not a popular view shared among theologians and Bible teachers. I had learned from Biblical teachings that God had made the sun, moon and stars on the 4th day. However, God continued to impress on my heart that this was not accurate. It took me several weeks and months to consider God's view. On one particular day I found the Old Hebrew time measurement and saw that their day actually began at 6pm and ends at 6pm (24 hours). Subsequently, the Old Hebrew 6pm is equivalent to our 12am and their 6am is equivalent to our 12pm (as shown in Table 1 below). As the Bible was originally written in Hebrew, it was evident to me that God began the recreation of the heavens and the earth at precisely 6pm!

Table 1 – Old Hebrew time vs. GMT time

		Greenwich Mean Time (GMT)/Our Time Scale							
		06.00am	07.00 am	08.00 am	09.00 am	10.00 am	11.00 am	12.00 am	01.00 am
Old Hebrew Time Scale	12.00pm								
	01.00pm								
	02.00pm								
	03.00pm								
	04.00pm								
	05.00pm								
	06.00pm							Genesis	
	07.00pm								

Synchronically, as 6pm – 6am is evening in Old Hebrew and 6am – 6pm is morning in Old Hebrew. Just as well, 12am - 12pm is morning in Greenwich Mean Time (GMT) and 12pm – 12am is evening in Greenwich Mean Time (GMT). These comparisons of the Old Hebrew 6pm coinciding with GMT 12am, creates a stark contrast, as we will later find in Table 2.

All through the 1st chapter of Genesis, the scripture continually prioritise evening before morning.

Examples are Genesis 1:5b, 8b, 13, 19, 23 and 31

V.s. 5b state: "… And the evening and the morning were the first day"

V.s. 8b state: "… And the evening and the morning were the second day"

V.s. 13 state: "And the evening and the morning were the third day"

V.s. 19 state: "And the evening and the morning were the fourth day"

V.s. 23 state: "And the evening and the morning were the fifth day"

V.s. 31 state: "And the evening and the morning were the sixth day"

Consequentially, evening in the Old Hebrew scriptures is depicted as morning and morning in the Old Hebrew scriptures is depicted as evening (but why?).

Table 2 - God's calculation of the 7 days of Genesis

Morning and Evening	M	E	M	E	M	E	M	E
Our calculation of day and night		1		2		3		4
God's calculation of day and night				1		2		3

As shown in Table 2, our 4th day coincides with God's 3rd day! This means we are a day behind God or at least 12 –18 hours behind (so therefore, either 6am – 6pm or 12am - 6pm is

160

missing from the start of creation). While meditating on this astounding revelation, I had secretly thought in my mind that God was somewhat gloomy for calculating creation days from evening instead of day, but then he made me see Genesis from his view. He explained to me (what I should have already known) that before he first appeared, there was no light or day. This is why he began to count from evening and night to day. I was saddened as I heard him speak to me because I did not wholly believe the literal account of Genesis all this while. He was the first light of day; nonetheless, he cannot be substituted as a function of day because he hopes that his presence 'as the creator' will be acknowledged at the beginning of creation. Nothing hurts him more than our unbelief because it makes him appear as a liar when he is not.

It was important to God that I understood this truth because of the revelation he had given me in volume 2 regarding the sun, moon and stars. God created the sun, moon and stars on the third day because they are to serve as the signature and ambassador of the Holy Trinity!

IS GENESIS 1, 2 OR 3?

THE FIRST GENESIS

According to the book of 2 Peter 3:5–7, a previous world had existed before our present world: *'For this they willingly are ignorant of, that by the word of God the heavens were of old, and the earth standing out of the water and in the water: whereby* **the world that then was, being overflowed with water, perished. But the heavens and the earth, which are now, by the same word are kept in store…'** Though some assume that this scripture is referring to the global flood in the days of Noah, other Biblical texts support the notion of a pre-existing world before Adam and Eve. God's primary purpose for creating the heavens and the earth was for inhabiting (Isaiah 45:18). However, after the first verse of Genesis one: *'In the beginning God created the heaven and the earth'*, verse two recorded that the earth was found empty and void. Naturally, there is an umbilical cord between creation and order but something aberrational must have transpired between Genesis 1:1 and Genesis 1:2.

The book of Isaiah 24:1, 3-4 sheds light on this matter:

162

'Behold, the Lord maketh the earth empty, and maketh it waste, **_and turneth it upside down_**, and scattereth abroad the inhabitants thereof. The land shall be utterly emptied, and utterly spoiled: for the Lord hath spoken this word. The earth mourneth and fadeth away, the world languisheth and fadeth away, the haughty people of the earth do languish.'

Also, Jeremiah 4:23-28 adds: '*I beheld the earth and lo, it was without form and void; and the heavens, and they had no light* [this was also recorded in Genesis 1:2]. *I beheld the mountains, and, lo, they trembled, and all the hills moved lightly. I beheld, and, lo, there was no man, and all the birds of the heavens were fled* [this suggests that there were previous inhabitants in the earth, similar to human and birds before the event of creation that's recorded in Genesis 1:2]. *I beheld, and, lo, the fruitful place was a wilderness, and all the cities thereof were broken down at the presence of the LORD, and by his fierce anger. For thus hath the LORD said, the whole land shall be desolate;* **_yet will I not make a full end_** [meaning a second earth was intended by God]. *For this shall the earth mourn, and the heavens above be black* [meaning there were no days or sunlight during this period]...'

Contrary to the global flood in the days of Noah, Genesis 7:12 reveal that there were days (sunlight) during Noah's flood, which means the flood in Genesis is different to that of Noah's. The book of Job also affirms this pre-historic event and tells how God shook the earth out of its ordained boundaries and extinguished the fire of the sun and stars in order to discontinue their functionality.

Job 9:2-8: '*I know it is so of a truth: but how should man be just with God? If he will contend with him, he cannot answer him one of a thousand. He* [God] *is wise in heart, and mighty in strength: who hath hardened himself against him* [God], *and hath prospered? Who removeth the mountains, and they know not: who overturneth them in his anger.* **Who shaketh the earth out of her place,** *and the pillars thereof tremble.* **Who commandeth the sun, and it riseth not; and sealeth up the stars.** *Who alone spreadeth out the heavens, and treadeth upon the waves of the sea.*'

From examining these verses, it is evident that a world existed before our world and this world also had a beginning. The creation of the world before ours, consisting of angels and beings (like humans) and other life forms represent the first Genesis. The narrative of Genesis 1:2-31 is a recreation story. There was a pre-existing earth buried in the deep (according to Genesis 1:2) and another earth was uncovered according to Genesis 1:9-10. By identifying these two earths in the first chapter of Genesis, the scripture shows that one was before the first day of our Genesis and the other was recreated during the second genesis – which is the beginning of our world.

In addition, because the earth was turned upside down and shaken out of its natural ordained boundary (according to Isaiah 24:1 and Job 9:5-6) one of the following insights illuminates the scientific mystery behind the eroded surface of planet Mars: 1. Either earth's neighbour – 'Mars' was the previous earth that was flooded and turned upside down (which is why Mars has a substantial evidence of a global flood). 2. Either Mars was affected by the turbulent flooding and shaking of its neighbour – 'earth' and consequently, portrays (till this day) a monumental evidence for the global flooding of the former earth in the pre-Adamic era. The scripture indicates the latter.

While secular scientists argue the age of the earth is billions of years old, creation scientists believe the earth is six thousand years young. Surprisingly, the scripture confirms that both are partly right. The earth is as old as Lucifer and as young as Adam and Eve. There were two Eden gardens recorded in the scriptures. The garden Lucifer walked in (Ezekiel 28:12-19), and the garden Adam and Eve walked in (Genesis 2:8). Ezekiel 28:13-14 describes a brief historical account of angel Lucifer: *'Thou hast been in Eden the garden of God; every precious stone was thy covering, the sardius, topaz and the diamond, the beryl, the onyx, and the jasper, the sapphire, the emerald and the carbuncle, and gold: the workmanship of thy tabrets and of thy pipes was prepared in thee in the day that thou wast created. Thou art the anointed cherub....'*

Please note in passing that Lucifer was created in daylight, meaning under the sun. Genesis 2:7-8 also discloses the beginning of Adam: *'And the Lord God formed man of the dust of the ground, and breathed into his nostrils the breath of life; and man became a living soul. And the Lord God planted a garden eastward in Eden; and there he put the man whom he had formed.'* As evidently shown from this verse of scripture, God had planted a new garden for Adam also in Eden.

The reason it has been difficult for many of us to determine the age of the heavens and the earth is because we tend to focus more on the creation than the creator. God made the heavens and the earth beside his own existence. He is both old and young. Infact, he is the oldest of all that exists, whether visible or invisible, yet the youngest! Though he is before all things, he is not affected by time. God is forever young! I have often said to some stern friends of mine that they may be startled to find a baby-looking figure in pampers when they are first introduced to God in heaven. It is evidently clear that whoever made the cosmos and our planet earth is incredibly imaginative and child-like. Matthew 19:14: '*But Jesus said, Suffer little children, and forbid them not, to come unto me: for of such is the kingdom of heaven.*'

THE SECOND AND THIRD
GENESIS

It is a widespread view that God created the world in six days and rested on the seventh. A closer look at the rainbow provides a compelling evidence for this Biblical account. We do not need a binocular or telescope to see how this could be true. The colours of the rainbow are the colours that make up the sun and they are seven in number. Every time we view the sun, which is the same as day, we are witnessing a symbolic representation for the Genesis story of creation.

.

Though the sun may appear to have one to three colours (orange, red and yellow), the falling rain unveils its true colours. Each colour of the rainbow – bent and reflected through droplets of rain, existentially originates from the sun and these seven colours systematically represent each day of creation. The rainbow vividly displays a riveting portrait of the second Genesis. (More on the second Genesis is expounded in the next chapter)

One of several reasons God created the rainbow is to uncover the truths of the second Genesis. Genesis chapters 6 and 7 record that a global flood visited the second earth after Noah finished building the ark that God instructed him to. New thunderous showers of rain poured through the open heavens during this flood, and after the flood, the earth was lit with the rainbow. The appearance of this first rainbow marked the beginning of a third Genesis, just as the appearance of the primordial light marked the beginning of the second Genesis! (Genesis 1:3).

In Genesis 9:12, the scripture narratively describes the origin of the rainbow: *'And God said, this is the token of the covenant which I make between me and you and every living creature that is with you, for perpetual generations.'* This means that the token of the covenant described in ensuing verses (as the rainbow) had been given to Noah and particularly - for future generations (i.e. you and I) as a covenant light that can reveal the mind of the creator and his covenant with creation. Verses 13-15 continues to expound on the token covenant, which is descriptively a rainbow: *'I do set my bow in the cloud and it shall be for a token of a covenant between me and earth. And it shall come to pass, when I bring a cloud* [rain] *over the earth, that the bow shall be seen in the cloud: And I will remember my covenant, which is between me and you...'*

Please note in passing that a devastating flood and the

appearance of a primordial light had preceded the second Genesis of the Adamic creation. Subsequently, another devastating flood and a primordial rainbow preceded a new beginning on the Adamic earth. And this was the third Genesis.

The global features of flood and light pioneered both the reign of Adam and Noah and God told Noah the same thing he had said to Adam after Adam was created. Genesis 1:28 to Adam, and Genesis 9:1-2 to Noah both stated: *'Be fruitful, multiply and replenish the earth'.* Conjointly, the biblical account of the second and third Genesis is characterized with the following: a flood to annihilate and end a previous world, moving waters/rain to mark the beginning of another world and a covenant light to activate the new world!

Furthermore, the rainbow is not merely an arc of light but is seen as an arc if standing on the surface of the earth, due to a lower altitude and horizon. At a higher altitude (in the sky) we would find that a rainbow is actually a circle of light.

In Isaiah 40:22, the scripture states the following: *'It is he that sitteth upon the circle of the earth…'* In Genesis 1:3, we find that the primordial light of God which first appeared in primal beginning could not have been the sun, moon or stars because the sun, moon and stars were not recreated until much later (Genesis 1:14).

Since the earth is circular in shape, each colour of the rainbow that sits across the circular earth is represented by a circle of light. And these collective lights are a contemporary expression of the primordial light of God, which first appeared on the pre-Adamic earth in the second Genesis.

Also, the number '7' is the only invariable feature on our calendar. A night is seldom 12 hours and a day is seldom 12 hours. To find an exact 12 hours of night and 12 hours of days in a 24 hour period is rare. Scientists have confirmed that a night and day of equal length (i.e. 12 hours each) may occur only twice a year, which is known as an equinox.

A month is another variable feature on our calendar, some are 30 days or 31 and February is often 28 days or 29 every fourth year. Because of February's variance in days every fourth year, a year is also another variable feature on our calendar; it is sometimes 365 or 366 days. The only invariably permanent feature on our calendar is a week – 'the 7 days' period that's synonymous with the Biblical account of creation (selah – pause and think).

So then, did God create the Adamic world in 7 days?

Evidently, he did! Everyday under the sun is a reminder that he did. It is also written in the rainbow.

GENESIS CHAPTERS 1 & 2

(Exploring the 2nd Genesis)

Genesis 1:2–3

_____

'And the earth was without form, and void; and darkness was upon the face of the deep. And the Spirit of God moved upon the face of the waters. And God said, Let there be light: and there was light.'

Before the primordial light appeared on the stage of creation in Genesis, the scriptures admit the presence of the Spirit and waters in pitch darkness. It is the combination of these three: Spirit, Water and Light that initiated the activities of creation. Though the waters were inactive until the descent of the Spirit and Light, it was the moving waters that preceded every other act of creation. The aggregation of the Spirit, Water and Light before the first day of our Adamic creation is the first expression of the triune deity and the Biblical cosmological foundation for creation.

Genesis 1: 4-5

_____

'*And God saw the light, that it was good: and God divided the light from darkness. And God called the light Day, and the darkness he called Night. And the evening and the morning were the first day*'

In the ensuing verses of 4 & 5, the forming earth began to rotate in front of, and away from, the still primordial light of God, which created a framework for night and day. This creative act was the beginning of time! As light alone could not create the concept of time for earth, darkness was passively created by God (please note in passing that darkness is only an absence of light, as cold is the absence of heat). So then, the co-existence of darkness with light is what created night and day and the reason for the night was to establish a representation for the function of the moon (the extraterrestrial symbol of our lord Jesus) and stars (the celestial symbol of the Holy Ghost).

Additionally, it is because of the pitch darkness of the night that we can recognise the moon as moonlight and discover hundreds of billions of stars. In heaven, there is neither night nor darkness (Revelation 22:5). In fact, light without night is the biblical depiction of heaven. God could have created the earth in the same way as he created heaven but deliberately chose not to. Without the passive creation of darkness and a need for the moonlight and stars, the divine revelation of the Holy trinity would have been hidden from our understanding. As previously shown in the second volume, the moon and stars epitomise a representation for the other two members of the Godhead.

Also, the creation of time in the fourth and fifth verses of Genesis marked the beginning of the first day of creation. However, this was only the beginning of the first day since time itself had just begun. Time is also a part of creation.

As we saw in verses 2 & 3 of Genesis 1, the primordial light which existed before time and in timelessness had initiated the process of creation but it wasn't until God created the systemic framework for night and day that time actually began.

God allocated boundaries between darkness and light as a dichotomy for night and day so as to create a need for the function of the stars, moon and sun, which evidently allude to the creator of Genesis as having a tripartite entity.

Genesis 1: 6-7

_____

'And God said, Let there be a firmament in the midst of the waters, and let it divide the waters from the waters. And God made the firmament, and divided the waters which were under the firmament from the waters which were above the firmament: and it was so.'

As a continuing act on the first day of creation, the scriptures record that God created a firmament (i.e. sky) in the midst of the waters. Verse 7 concedes that there were waters above the firmament and waters under the firmament, which makes the firmament (sky) in-between the waters a third division in the creative act of God. The creation of the sky between the waters above and under allowed the following:

1. Space for the waters above the firmament

2. Space for the waters under the firmament

3. Space for the moist and misty clouds between 1 & 2

These three divisions convey yet another vivid portrait for the Holy Trinity.

In the later verses of 8, 9 & 10, God commanded the waters

under the firmament (i.e. on earth) to be gathered together in allocated boundaries (such as rivers, seas, oceans) and in several locations on the planet earth so as to uncover the dry surfaces of the earth. These dry surfaces and lands became the artistic canvas for God's continued acts of creation:

'And God called the firmament Heaven. And the evening and the morning were the second day. And God said, Let the waters under the heaven be gathered together unto one place, and let the dry land appear: and it was so. And God called the dry land Earth; and the gathering together of the waters called he Seas: and God saw that it was good.'

Also, this creative act was the beginning of the second day.

Genesis 1:11-12

'And God said, Let the earth bring forth **grass***, the* **herb yielding seed***, and the* **fruit tree yielding** *fruit after his kind, whose seed is in itself, upon the earth: and it was so. And the earth brought forth grass and herb yielding seed after his kind, and the tree yielding fruit, whose seed was in itself, after his kind: and God saw that it was good.'*

The highlighted text on the second day of creation reveals yet another Trinitarian representation: Grass, Herb and Fruit.

Genesis 1:13-18

_____

'And the evening and the morning were the third day. And God said, Let there be lights in the firmament of the heaven to divide the day from the night; and let them be for signs, and for seasons, and for days and years: And let them be for lights in the firmament of the heaven to give light upon the earth: and it was so. And God made two great lights; **the greater light** [sun] **to rule the day, and the lesser light** [moon] **to rule the night: he made the stars also.** *And God set them in the firmament of the heaven to give light upon the earth, And* **to rule over the day and over the night, and to divide the light from the darkness** [meaning to create time]*: and God saw that it was good.'*

As illustrated in the second volume of this book, the sun, moon and stars are cosmic symbols of the Holy Trinity and were re-created on the third day of Genesis to rule over night and day. Verses 16 and 18 further illustrates that time was created on the first day of Genesis for the representation of these three embodiments of lights and their purpose to serve as representatives for the Holy Trinity.

Genesis 1: 19 – 22

'And the evening and the morning were the fourth day. And God said, let the **waters bring forth abundantly the moving creature that hath life,** *and* **fowl that may fly above the earth in the open firmament of heaven.** *And God created great whales, and every living creature that moveth, which the waters brought forth abundantly, after their kind,* **and every winged fowl after his kind:** *and God saw that it was good. And God blessed them, saying, Be fruitful, and multiply, and fill the waters in the seas, and let fowl multiply in the earth.'*

Again, on the fourth day of creation, the highlighted text above reveals yet another Trinitarian representation: moving creatures in the waters, fowls that fly in the air and the fowls on the dry ground that cannot fly.

Genesis 1: 23 – 25

---

*'And the evening and the morning were the fifth day. And God said, Let the earth bring forth the living creature after his kind, **cattle**, and **creeping thing**, and **beast of the earth** after his kind: and it was so. And God made the beast of the earth after his kind, and cattle after their kind, and every thing that creepeth upon the earth after his kind: and God saw that it was good.'*

On the fifth day of creation, we find from the highlighted text above yet another Trinitarian representation: cattle, creeping creatures and the beast of the earth.

Genesis 1: 26 – 31

'And God said, "Let us" make man in our image, after our likeness and let them have dominion over the fish of the sea, and over the fowl of the air, and over the cattle, and over all the earth, and over every creeping thing that creepeth upon the earth. So God created man in his own image, in the image of God created he him; male and female created he them. And God blessed them, and God said unto them, Be fruitful, and multiply, and replenish the earth, and subdue it: and have dominion over the fish of the sea, and over the fowl of the air, and over every living thing that moveth upon the earth. And God

said, Behold, I have given you every herb bearing seed, which is upon the face of all the earth, and every tree, in the which is the fruit of a tree yielding seed; to you it shall be for meat. And to every beast of the earth, and to every fowl of the air, and to every thing that creepeth upon the earth, wherein there is life, I have given every green herb for meat and it was so. And God saw every thing that he had made, and, behold, it was very good. And the evening and the morning were the sixth day.'

On the sixth day of creation, God identified himself as a united plural deity and made humans a trinity like the Holy Trinity! (We shall revisit this subject of the trinity of humanity in my next book). The underlying principle and concept of a triune entity in Genesis 1 resurfaced in the story of Adam and Eve in Genesis chapter 2. Like the triune deity, God intended that Adam and Eve would be one as they are. In Genesis 2:24, the scripture states *'Therefore shall a man leave his father and his mother, and shall cleave unto his wife: and they shall be one flesh.'* One may question the intelligence behind this statement. How can two persons become one? The mathematical formula that God first mentioned to Adam and Eve in Genesis 1:28 makes this possible *'...Be fruitful and "multiply"...'* 2 can become 1 either through division (1/1 = 1) or multiplication. Since God is referring to the unity of two for the purpose of reproduction and self-perpetuating, the obvious inference is multiplication (1x1=1). We will find in Genesis that God always addressed Adam and Eve as one and also named them both Adam (Genesis 5:2). And just as 1 x 1 = 1, likewise 1 x 1 x 1 = 1.

Genesis 2: 1 – 3

––––––––––––––

'Thus the heavens and the earth were finished, and all the host of them. And on the seventh day God ended his work which he had made; and he rested on the seventh day from all his work which he had made. And God blessed the seventh day, and sanctified it: because that in it he had rested from all his work which God created and made.'

Genesis chapter one illustrates that God created everything in threes and this Biblical clue helps us realise that God was present in Genesis as a triune deity. (Please note in passing that Genesis 1 is an overview summary of creation while Genesis 2 sheds more light on the intricacies of Genesis 1).

Furthermore, since night and day began before the making of

the sun, moon and stars, the light before the first day of creation could not have been the same as the sun, moon and stars. God began counting the days of creation before remaking the solar lights on the 3rd day so we do not ascribe his sovereign power to the celestial lights but instead, to the creator God who had made them. The scripture explicitly forbids the worship of celestial lights in Deuteronomy 4:19 and Deuteronomy 17:3. Additionally, the primordial light in Genesis was the temporary light (in the absence of the sun) that empowered and engineered the potential growth in *the herb yielding seed and the tree yielding fruit, whose seed was in itself* on the second day of creation. (More on this primordial light is revealed in the third volume).

God did not have to create the second heavens and the second earth in 7 days; he has always been powerful enough to create anything and everything in a split of a nano second. Till date, many assume to know the actual days that God spent to create the heavens and the earth, but nobody really knows of the first heavens and earth, they only know of the second. Knowing God as I now do, I believe he may have spent a lot longer than many of us would imagine. The story of Genesis was never about power but about the demonstration of God's love toward creation and humans are the masterpieces of his creative artistry. A lot of imagination, thinking, planning and patience must have been invested in the creative process of Genesis, which indicates that God esteems love above power and character above his self-pride. (Please note that God actually plans, thinks and has thoughts before acting, many forget how true this is. Psalm 92:5 and Jeremiah 29:11)

The recreation of the heavens and the earth in the second Genesis required deliberate and careful planning, it required preliminary, conceptual and realisation designs. 'Preliminary' because God created everything in preparatory stages, 'conceptual' because God created multiple diversities and varieties in view of achieving a uniformed and singular goal, and 'realisation' because after every stage of creation, God paused and reflected to see how well things had come together. He expressed on all six stages of creation that what he had created and made looked good! On the eve of the 7th day, he particularly expressed that it was all very good! (Genesis 1:4, 10, 12, 18, 21, 25 and 31).

He made everything else before making us and did not make anything else after he made humans. It was all for us as it is for his pleasure (Genesis 1:27-28, Revelation 4:11). As Jesus was predestined to become a human deity (humanity existing before human creation), it was feasible to make a world that was conveniently accommodating for humans, it was through the eyes of Jesus that the Father God knew that what he had made for humans looked good!

He made it all to impress us, which is why we were the last of his creation and the youngest as well. The blue oceans, the lilies and flowers, the landscapes and vegetations, the mountains and hills, the valleys, birds and fishes, the skies and the evergreens were all made for us through the eyes of Jesus. God made us at the end of it all because he wanted everything in place before we got here and wanted our stay on earth to be pleasurable and exciting. What a God! What a loving Father! Animals cannot appreciate the colours in the sky, it was not primarily made for them, they cannot draw, paint or animate the images of the blue skies or the orange sunsets, they cannot travel to the moon or read and write poems about it. They cannot encapsulate the visions of galaxies and the cosmos or appreciate the sentiments of a rainbow but we can, we can. Humans are the pinnacle on God's creative pedestal.

God essentially made the earth in 6 days (Exodus 20:11) but included a 7th so we can remember to acknowledge him as the creator of the creation in the 6 days period (this was also the reason for the Sabbath law in the scriptures). The scriptures could have stated that God went up to heaven to rest for aeons and aeons of years, but intentionally stated that God rested on the 7th day so the number 7 can become a numerical metaphor to communicate a divine symbol for completion and perfection.

Some have questioned if God had rested on planet earth or in heaven after the six days of creation. However, the seventh day was not solely about resting. If it was, then we should also acknowledge the 8th day as God's day of rest or the 9th day, the 10th and so on. Isaiah 66:1-2 reports: *'Thus saith the Lord, the heaven is my throne, and the earth is my footstool: where is the house that ye build unto me? And **where is the place of my rest? For all those things hath mine hand made...***'*

It is evident that since the six days of creation, God has been resting from the event of creation. The chief purpose of the 7th day and 7 days is to remind us to acknowledge God as our creator. Seven is a number that has now become intrinsic in communicating this divine truth to us and is apparent in the constant and fixed number of days in a week. God often choose to speak to us through numbers because numbers epitomise order and add meaning to our day to day living. Almost everything of significance in the human life is a subject of number: weight, height, money, dates, age, time, anniversaries, birthdays, clothe sizes, blood count and book pages e.t.c.

One of the first five books in the scriptures is titled 'Numbers' and every letter of the Biblical Hebrew alphabet has numerical value. As shown in the third Genesis, the seven colours of the rainbow were created by God to convey a new covenant with creation and to confirm the days of our Genesis.

GENESIS CHAPTER 3

A while ago, a friend and I were discussing the likelihood of finding the perfect soul mate. As we continued talking, the story of Adam and Eve came to mind, so I made mention of their names in our conversation to deduce a sexual inference from this Biblical text. Eve is described in the Bible as the flesh of Adam's flesh and the bone of his bone. As a single guy, that got me excited.

My friend had placed more emphasis on the spiritual element of this narrative, which was boring to me at the time. I had always assumed almost everybody knew the story well, but then it struck me that I did not know nearly enough. I remember my friend had expressed his romantic aspiration to find eternal bliss with 'the perfect woman' that God had chosen for him but his expression gave me a sudden fright! It reminded me of the factual story of Adam and Eve.

As narrated in Genesis, Adam was hand-made and created from the earth by God and Eve was hand-made and created from Adam's rib for Adam, yet their relationship evolved into many terrible losses. They lost their first home and kingdom; they lost their second son to a crime of murder by their first child and also lost their first child to a nomadic living. They endured much suffering until their death, though neither sufferings nor death was God's original intention for creating them.

Adam was (directly) given an instruction from God not *to eat from the forbidden tree* but later disobeyed and consequently, lost almost everything he had been given from God.

As Genesis 3:16-19 shows, when God addressed Eve after her disobedience, God did not mention the instruction he had given, but only made reference to it when speaking to Adam. It is covertly shown in Genesis 3:2-3 that Eve may have received this instruction from Adam and not God.

In her conversation with the serpent, she alleges that God said *not to eat from the forbidden tree nor touch it,* but God did not say to Adam *not to touch the tree or fruit.* Eve's reply to the serpent at this time seemed honest. She had said this in the presence of Adam and Adam did not dispute it! (Genesis 3:6b revealed that Adam was with Eve during her conversation with the serpent).

Not to eat from the forbidden tree was the exact instruction that God gave to Adam (recorded in Genesis 2:17 and Genesis 3:17) but somewhere, somehow, the original instruction had become distorted and exaggerated between Adam and Eve.

189

ADAM & EVE - *What happened?*

Find out in my book – The Mystery

VOLUME 3

Verily thou art a God that hidest thyself...'

Isaiah 45:15

WATER

We are all water creatures, whether living in water or waters

living in us

The Gap Theory

Take a second look at the image on the left hand corner. It is similar to what I experienced 20 something years ago. I am not a diver or swimmer, I have never been inside a whale, but I know what it feels like.

It must have been between the ages of three and nine when I had a strange visitor at my home. I was not standing beside an ocean or lake, I was not in the shower or bath tub, I was standing in a furnished living room when suddenly, a wide stream of water and a man in a diver suit appeared on the long narrow corridor that faced the living room. I have played this over and over again in my head to see if I was really awake or dreaming. Till this day, I cannot tell but I know it happened!

I kept this supernatural encounter discreet for many years because I never understood it and was frightened by it. Consequently, I forgot it altogether, until 2009 when I began to examine the text in Genesis 1:2 - *And the earth was without form, and void; and darkness was upon the face of the deep. And the Spirit of God moved upon the face of the waters.* How is it that water preceded the event of creation, and why is there no explicit reference for the origin of water? Of course, we find references for 'the gathering of waters' (Genesis 1:10) – the rivers, lakes, seas and oceans. However, there is no succinct description for the emergence of water. Water, according to Genesis, existed before the descent of God's spirit and light, before time and every other activity of creation.

Intrigued? I am.

I cannot remember if the diver I had encountered many years back had said anything to me. He seemed to be unaware of my frightful state and existence – like a cable man who had come to install a dish in a family home, he wasn't oblivious of his surroundings, yet he barely acknowledged I was present. As he walked toward the living room (where I was), I instinctively ran for cover but every step he took channelled a strong current of unseen water that restricted my motion. I managed to push through and hid my face and upper body under the arm rest of a three-seat sofa. But before I could pull in my lower body, the visitor was in my living room and I was unable to move. It felt at this time, like my entire body was quickly swallowed and engulfed in deep waters, yet I could not feel the moistness or touch of water. My clothes were dry, they were not dampened or soaked, yet I felt like I was in the heart of the ocean. I was terrified, crying and calling for my absent mother and calling on God for rescue. I could move my lips but could not move any other part of my body. I observed that the air around me was frozen still; it was as though the motion of time had temporarily stopped.

I am not sure what followed after this. I only remember the following from what I encountered on that day, and of course, these three: A mysterious masked diver, water and frozen time.

There is a gap in knowledge between the first and second verse of Genesis chapter one. Theologians often refer to this gap as the 'Gap Theory'. After God 'created' the heaven and the earth as recorded in Genesis 1:1 - synonymous with order, form and shape. The second verse of Genesis begins with an antithetic portrait of creation '*And the earth was without form and void…*' What caused the previously created earth to become formless and void is not revealed to us in the text of Genesis. However, other biblical text informs us sparingly.

The Apostle John (surrealistically) contributes to bridge the gap between Genesis 1:1 and 2 by pairing the incidence of the death of Jesus with the beginning of our world. Most certainly, John was entranced in a spiritual ecstasy (Revelation 1:10) when he saw *the lamb* [Jesus] *that was slain from the foundation of the world* (Revelation 13:8). The scripture records that John was physically present at the crucifixion of Jesus on the cross (John 19:26-27) but he could not have been physically present at the beginning of our world. So how is it possible that John knew this?

(In the human mind, the earthly dimension appears more real than the supernatural – which we mentally see as abstractions and imaginations. Whereas, in the mind of the spirit, the supernatural dimension is an idea that concurrently co-exists with reality. Invariably, the spirit of God envisions the earthly dimension as a finite temporal manifestation from the infinite divine. This implies that what exist has already been. In this case, the lamb - Christ Jesus, was slain from the foundation of creation! It follows then, that what John saw 'through the mind of the spirit' – that is, the death of Jesus before our world began was seen in a symbolic form and pattern.)

Though John had previously witnessed the physical and human death of Jesus in 'an earthly dimension', he later saw that the same incidence had transpired in 'a supernatural dimension'. Remarkably, John's vision coincided with the letter written by the Apostle Paul to the Ephesians church, who also expressed through divine inspiration that God *hath chosen us in him* [Jesus] *before the foundation of the world...* (Ephesians 1:4). But what could all these Biblical verse(s) metaphorically or literally mean?? (Some may ask).

Ever so often, Bible critics criticise the poetic style of Biblical writing, deeming it elusive and unreal because it seldom reads like an historical non-fiction. They are partly right. God cannot be fully expressed in a realistic dimension because he exists in a surrealistic dimension (Psalms 115:16). Due to the fall of Adam and the ensuing consequences inherited in nature, our earthly dimension is not as advanced as God's.

While we reside in a fallen earth, God resides in heaven. Indeed, we are real but God is super real. Therefore, a poetic language capable of being transcendent and ubiquitous in style will serve effectively in translating God's thoughts and sayings to us. Additionally, because our reach for God naturally exceeds our grasp of God, a poetic and metaphoric language is often necessary.

Put simply and succinctly, it stands to reason that we embrace a literature style that can help to facilitate intuitive meditation and quiet reflection, so as to comprehend and absorb the infinite knowledge of God. (Joshua 1:8)

Returning to the outset of the second Genesis (The Adamic race), the scripture informs us that our world began in pitch darkness and with 'frozen ice' (Job 38:30 confirms this). Naturally, this would make sense because darkness can only exist in the absence of light and liquid water can also become frozen in the long absence of the heat radiation that comes from light.

To illuminate the visual context of Genesis 1:2, the image following correlatively displays a skeletal portrait. Though the earth was not at this time in its present spherical form and shape, there is an underlying descending order to uncover from its dark and chaotic surroundings.

Genesis 1:2 – *And the earth was without form, and void; and darkness was upon the* [Sur] *face of the deep. And the Spirit of God moved upon the* [Sur] *face of the water.*

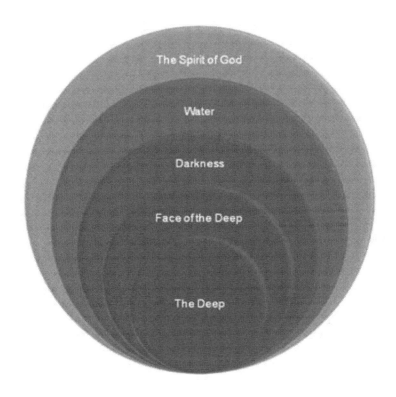

Sojourn with me a little on the theatrical stage of creation, where the lines between the supernatural and natural are constantly blurred. Sadly, the finite mind may view this in light of metaphors and mental abstractions. But at the end of this tour, we shall find the literal meaning behind the poetic and rhythmical words of God.

A taxonomical observation of the primal conditions of the pre-existing earth places 'The Deep' at the centre core and undermost layer of the earth, and 'The Spirit of God' at the circumference and uppermost layer of the earth. The deep is often characterised in the narratives of the scriptures as the underworld of demons and fallen angels. The face of the deep, which extends to the surface of the earth, consists of the bodies of rivers and oceans, clay, mud, dusts, the buried dead and buried fossils. The darkness (same as absence of light and a shadow of the face of the deep in this instance) is symbolic of the fallen human race, which were introduced to the world through the loins of Adam and Eve. The waters, compassed with darkness, and spread over the surface of the earth is symbolic of Jesus, the son of man who laid his life on the cross to save the Adamic race and creation. In addition, because water can get into places that air cannot, and can soak through hard surfaces including rocks and stones – the waters, according to Genesis, soaked through its outermost boundaries on the surface of the earth, and was also present on the face of the deep. Finally, the Spirit of God (also known as the Holy Ghost) was the only moving and living entity on the lifeless and primal stage of creation. The Holy Spirit, according to Genesis was the first to descend on the wasted earth, bringing life to its death (Psalms 104:30). In the New Testament, the Holy Spirit also raised Jesus from the dead.

To appease the Biblical astute and Bible critics, we shall try to examine these five components of primal pre-creation independently.

First - "The Deep": In Luke 8:30-31, a dialogue with Jesus reveals it's meaning to us *'And Jesus asked him, saying, What is thy name? And he said Legion: because many devils were entered into him. And they besought him that he would not command them to go out into the deep.'* Revelation 9:2 also reveals the climatic nature of the deep: *'And he opened the bottomless pit; and there arose a smoke out of the pit, as the smoke of a great furnace...'* Revelation 20:3 adds *'And he laid hold on the dragon, that old serpent, which is the devil, and satan, and bound him a thousand years, and cast him into the bottomless pit, and shut him up, and set a seal upon him, that he should deceive the nations no more...'* . Evidently, 'the deep' is depicted in these verses of scripture as a 'sealed and covered furnace'. It is also known as the bottomless pit, hades or hell. Slightly different to the image above, the deep is not located at the very bottom of the earth but in its centre core. If the earth was a square or rectangle, the deep would have had a bottom but because the earth is circular, the deep is without a bottom and as such, bottomless. It is located in the heart of the earth. Jesus also confirms this precise location when he spoke of his three days death and descent into hell in Matthew 12:40 *'For as Jonas was three days and three nights in the whale's belly; so shall the Son of man be three days and three nights in the heart of the earth.'*

Second – "The face of the Deep": In Proverbs 8:25-27, the scripture reveals the location of the face of the deep as beneath the surface of the earth *'Before the mountains were settled, before the hills was I* [God's Wisdom] *brought forth: While as yet he had not made the earth, nor the fields, nor the highest part of the dust of the world* [i.e. the outermost surface of the earth]. *When he prepared the heavens, I* [God's Wisdom] *was there: **when he set a compass*** [meaning a surrounding circle] ***upon the face of the depth.'*** The ESV Bible translates this last line more succinctly *'...when he drew a circle on the face of the deep.'* Clearly, we find from this verse of scripture that a vertical and horizontal equidistance exist between the surface of the earth and the face of the deep. In the following verse (Vs 28) the scripture also mentions *'the fountains of the deep'* – which are the liquid body of oceans, rivers and lakes. Their surfaces, however, are the same as the surface of the earth. And between the face of the deep and the surface of the earth is also where the dead are buried and where fossils are unearthed.

Third – "Darkness": In John 12:46, the scripture reveals the symbolic meaning of darkness: *'I [Jesus] have come as a light to the* **world**, *that whoever believes in me should not abide in* **darkness**.*'* This verse correlatively implies that darkness is the world of humanity. The Psalmist shed more light on this in Psalm 51:5-6 *'Behold, I was shapen in iniquity; and in sin did my mother conceive me. Behold thou [God] desires truth in the inward parts: and in the hidden part...'* Ephesians 5:8, a letter to the Ephesians church adds: *'For you were sometimes darkness, but now are you light in the lord...'* Symbolically, the darkness in Genesis represents the fallen human race, who inherited the sinful nature of the first man and woman.

Because of Adam and Eve's disobedience to God, the ensuing descendants of humanity from their union, and all of earth's creation, which were originally created to serve Adam and Eve (Genesis 1:26-30) became predisposed to follow in the same path, and fall in the same pit ('the deep') as the previous generations. The darkness on the outset of Genesis was the shadow of 'the deep': as it is the influence of Satan, the old serpent from the abyss of the deep (recorded in Revelation 12:9) that was embodied in a serpent at the Garden of Eden and tempted Adam and Eve to disobey God, and to suffer the consequences for their disobedience. John 3:19 expounds *'… the light is come into the world, and men loved darkness rather than light…'*

Fourth – "Waters": In several passages of the scriptures, water is covertly affiliated and interchangeably used as a representation for the word of God: which is also the name of Christ Jesus (Revelation 19:13). Whether it's the written or spoken word of God, Jesus was and is the incarnated word of God (John 1:1-3). An example of this intimate association between the word and water can be found in Ephesians 5:26 *'That he might sanctify and cleanse it with the washing of water by the word.'* John 17:17 adds: *'Sanctify them through thy truth: thy word is truth.'* And John 14:6 *'Jesus saith unto him, I am the way, the truth and the life: no man comes to the Father but by me.'* We shall revisit the Biblical narratives on water and its inherent relation to Jesus Christ as we continue.

Fifth – "The Spirit of God": The Spirit of God is the Holy Spirit in the Old Testament and is alternatively known as the "Holy Ghost" in the New Testament because of the resurrection of Christ Jesus. Romans 8:11 reveals the hidden meaning behind the new identity of the Spirit. *'But if the Spirit of him* [the Father] *that raised up Jesus from the dead* [Holy Ghost] *dwell in you, he that raised up Christ from the dead shall also quicken your mortal bodies by his Spirit that dwelleth in you.'*

'Repetition is the mother of learning'

- White Mountain Apache Indians Archives

In Genesis 1:1, we find a Biblical premise for the beginning of the first creation. However, Genesis 1:2 (the gap theory) is the beginning of the second creation, which we are a part of.

The prehistoric evidence for the creation of the world before ours can be seen at the creation of our world. Just as the Spirit, water and light preceded the beginning of our world, similarly, it is the Spirit, water and light that preceded the creation of the world before. The book of 2 Peter 3:5-7 compares the architectural structure of the first earth to our present earth. *'For this they willingly are ignorant of, that by the word of God the* [first] *heavens were of old* [i.e. it became prehistoric, and the same is true for the first earth], *and the* [first] *earth standing out of the water* [meaning its dry regions and surfaces] *and in the water* [meaning the dry earth was surrounded and compassed mostly by water - rivers, seas, lakes and oceans, just as we find in the global surroundings of our present earth]: *Whereby the world that then was, being overflowed with water, perished* [again here, it suggests that the earth before our present earth was mostly water and surrounded with water. As such, the first earth, like the second earth, in the days of Noah, had the potential to become globally flooded]: *But the heavens and the earth, which are now* [referring to the present earth and heavens that was recreated in Genesis 1:2], *by the same word are kept in store...'*

As we find in the opening verses of Genesis, the origin of water is unexplained and seems to display an omnipresent invariance. Water first came to life in our Genesis before the process of recreation began, and that water is the witness of Jesus (1 John 5:7). Toward the end of the first earth, prior to the beginning of the second, is where the disobedience of creation toward the creator first began, it is also where death originated. It is from this preliminary stage that we can uncover the biblical mystery and revelation of Jesus (at the cross) as *the first born from the dead* - Colossians 1:18. Our world was founded on the cross of Jesus and as previously shown in the second volume; the symbol of the cross represents the 4 corners of the earth. Also, the gathered waters that remained on our planet earth during the course of creation was first divided by God into four river heads (Genesis 2:10-14). The earth is mainly water as it is dry land - Selah. The lyric of a famous song by Simon & Garfunke in the 1960's echoes the sound of redemption for humanity from the primal stage of creation *'When evening falls so hard, I will comfort you. I'll take your part when darkness comes. Like a bridge over troubled water, I will lay me down. Like a bridge over troubled water, I will lay me down.'* (these words figuratively conveys how Jesus took our place on the cross).

Furthermore, in the prehistoric event of the first creation (before the created heaven and earth in Genesis 1:1), water was present. And this water served as a witness for Christ Jesus, who is also described in the scripture as *the first born of all creation* (Colossians 1:15). Water also preceded the creation of Adam in Eden. Genesis 2:6-7 descriptively prioritize water as an integral pre-requisite to the formation of Adam, just as we find the precedence of water at the beginning of our cosmic creation – *But there went up a mist from the earth, and watered the whole face of the ground. And the lord God formed man of the dust of the ground...'* (The inference from this verse of scripture is that Jesus was before Adam as water is before Adam).

Resuming to 2 Peter 3:5-7, there was a pre-Adamic flood, and waters were present in the pre-Adamic earth - in quantities large enough to create a global flood. The similarity of the first earth and the second suggest that waters must have preceded the beginning of the first creation, as we find at the beginning of the second creation.

The book of Psalm 24:1-2 also confirms this notion: *'The earth is the Lord's and the fullness thereof; the world and they that dwell therein. For he hath founded it upon the seas, and established it upon the floods'*. This text evidently encompasses the narratives for the first and second earth's origin. The first earth was founded on a peaceful origin - hence, the scriptural reference for seas (water). And the second earth was founded on a destructive origin - hence, the scriptural reference for floods (water and other things).

The book of 1 John 5:6 also speaks volumes on this matter. In the first part of the text, it states: *This is he that came by water and blood, even Jesus Christ;* **not by water only,** *but by* **water and blood**. [The scripture here subtly differentiates 'water' from 'water and blood'. By excluding water, it is referring to the beginning of the first world, which was founded by Jesus on peaceful grounds. And by pairing water with blood, it is referring to the judgement and destruction of the first world, which preceded the foundation of our world.]

In the second part of 1 John 5:6, it states: ...*And it is the Spirit that beareth witness, because the Spirit is truth.* [this aspect of the scripture is referring to the eye witness and physical presence of the Holy Spirit in primal beginning. Genesis 1:2 records that the spirit of God moved on the face of the frozen waters, prior to the beginning of the Adamic world]

In addition, the revelation of the moon's astronomic narratives in the previous volume relates Jesus' 'shed blood' and 'water break' to 1 John 5:6. In a similar comparison, the gap theory (Genesis 1:2) is another Biblical evidence for the 'blood shed' and 'water break' of Jesus from the foundation of our world, and synchronises with Jesus' death on the cross in Israel. The book of John 19:34 records that water and blood came out of Jesus' wounded side after death.

Water was intrinsically created while other creations in Genesis were extrinsically created. And it is in this sense that water is the witness of Jesus (1 John 5:7-8). Other creation came from without, but water came from within, and just as Jesus stands between the Father and the Adamic world as the divine mediator, likewise, water stands before the creator and his creation. It is from water that all things emerged.

Our planet earth (mostly consisting of water) is often described by planet scientists as having a motherly characteristic (like a woman with child)! However, the primary inference from this description is the child; otherwise, planet earth will be described as a woman and not a mother. The reason planet earth and the human body are mostly water is for the symbolic witness of water's representation of Jesus as a son: who is also the creator of all creation.

The macrographic representation of water as a witness for Jesus – *the first born of every creature* (Colossians 1:15) concedes that Jesus' divine origin is biologically fulfilled in the birth of every child because prior to our human birth, water must first exit the womb of our pregnant mothers. And as we find water to be first born: likewise, Jesus is the first born of every creature!

We cannot easily discard the gospel of Jesus. It is not a side revelation or an alternative to life but compass a primary and basic necessity to human living. Just as crucial and ubiquitous as water is, so is Jesus. Water existed because of him. This is what the Bible implicitly proposes when it states that water is the witness of Jesus. Certainly, there are other witnesses that reflect the testimony of our lord but water is prepensely identified as a representation for him and his relationship with our planet earth.

This symbolic meaning of water is also the primary reason behind the doctrine and practice of water baptism in Christendom. It is a clever mystery to distinguish the creator of our existence from other gods. The doctrine of water baptism represents the birth of Jesus from the dead (at the cross and the beginning of the Adamic creation). Because all creation is first drawn out of water in our human birth, by the symbolic act of water baptism, we are physically identifying with a second birth. This is the underlying meaning of water baptism – to be born again! (John 3:3).

With the existence of water, we need not ask what God smells like or what colour of skin God has or what God tastes like - liquid water is proof of the divine to the diversified colours and ethnicities of humanity. Water is indispensable to life and inseparable from the living and although it is a witness of the immortal son of man – Christ Jesus, **it should neither be revered nor deified as the divine**. It's purpose as the cradle and womb of creation is to help us recognise 'the son of God', who existed before creation, and descended to earth in human form amid other look-alike creation, yet was not another human creature but the creator of all things.

On two occasions - in prehistory and history, water was used 'as a global witness' to establish God's Judgement in the earth. The first was the global flood in the pre-Adamic era and the second was in the days of Noah. However, the same water that executed God's judgement in the pre-adamic flood was also judged. The water of the pre-adamic flood was polluted with every horrific dead thing and buried frozen that it needed to be reborn. Similarly, Jesus was judged on our behalf from the beginning.

All universal judgement both in the world before and the world that now is has been committed by the Father to the Son and water is the witness of this transaction. John 5:22 reveals: *'For the Father judgeth no man, but hath committed all judgement unto the Son.'*

The first world as we find in the scriptures was annihilated and destroyed in the first flood. The second flood was chiefly purposed to eliminate the fallen angelic inhabitants of the pre-Adamic race, who descended to earth and mated with humans to create monstrous progenies (Genesis 6:2, 4). These fallen angels had devised a strategic scheme to encroach and infiltrate the human genetics, in order to remodel and remake the human creation in their own image and likeness.

This second flood occurred after several years of God impressing a moral responsibility on the human conscience (Genesis 6:3) and the heedless warnings from Noah to the people who lived in his days. (2 Peter 2:5, Genesis 6:1-22). However, God preserved the structure of the earth in the second flood, so its devastation was not as dire as the first.

The purpose of the second flood was to preserve the future of the Adamic human race, and to assist in perpetuating God's redemptive plan to bring salvation to humanity through the seed of a woman that was pure human (Genesis 3:15). If any human had paid attention to God's spirit or Noah by repenting and obeying the instructions from God, they would have not been destroyed in the flood (but God foreknew that none would repent).

God did not destroy the structure of the earth in the second flood, because his original intention was not to destroy the Adamic creation but to bring justice to the wickedness of the fallen angels and to put an end to their diabolical influence in the world of humanity.

Sadly, this dream could only be realised through the lineage of Noah (see 1 Peter 3:20b. Also Matthew 24:37). Noah found grace in the sight of God as we also have (Ephesians 2:8, Genesis 6:8)

INTERFACE: JOHN ONE

'You don't understand anything until you learn it more than one way.'

– Marvin Minsky

The 'frozen waters' in Genesis epitomized an actual 'dead sea'. Saturated and filled with the depleted and lifeless residues of pre-historic creation, the water had lost its life giving vitality and quality. It can be said that 'the water also died'... until God spoke!

The first expression of the Father (in Genesis 1:3) was the Son; this is why Jesus is often described in scriptures as the word of God. His name is 'The Word of God' - Revelation 19:13. The book of John chapter one puts it this way – *'In the beginning was the Word'*. And in the next line *'...and the Word was with God'*. John here identifies the Word as a person. *'...and the Word was God'* (How is this possible, you may ask?)

But let's read on. *'The same was in the beginning with God'* Here again, John has separated the identity of this person who is 'The Word' spoken by God but continues to maintain that this person is also God. *'All things were made by him; and without him was not any thing made that was made'*. Alright, let's pause here and recap. 'The word' (Christ Jesus) is a person with another person (Father God) and the word along with the Father God is the creator who made everything.

To shed more light on the narratives of John 1:1-3, let's compare what we have read so far with Genesis 1:2b and 3 *'...And the spirit of God moved upon the face of the waters. And God said, Let there be light: and there was light'*. The first light that appeared in Genesis was not a mere apparition of light but a physically embodied light: it was light absorbed in matter. Christ Jesus was physically present at the beginning of creation; and this should come as no surprise to us because the spirit of God was also there in person. The spirit of God was the primordial spirit that moved over the face of the frozen waters and Christ Jesus was the primordial light that manifested from the Father, who also gave life to the frozen waters and ultimately engendered creation.

The scriptures suggests that the first light that appeared in Genesis, and the spirit of God, were not part of the physical order of creation, but both are introduced in our cosmic Genesis as the divine catalyst that initiated the activities of creation. Every created entity and creation is part of the visible and physical order of creation and can be physically observed till this day, but the primordial spirit and primordial light appeared temporarily to oversee and enforce the activities of creation.

Furthermore, the Apostles John and Paul made an explicit reference for the death of Jesus at the foundation of our world. So therefore, an implicit reference for Jesus' resurrection should also be present in the narratives of Genesis. Genesis 1:2 is the biblical premise for Jesus' death and Genesis 1:3 is the biblical premise for his resurrection.

Concurrently, Jesus was present at the beginning as the frozen waters among the dead, and also as the pre-existing light that came from the Father to revive the dead and frozen waters – which represents his wasted and lifeless human body at the cross.

Jesus' human resurrection was initiated by the first light in Genesis (his divine self) that came from the Father. When the warm rays of the primordial light met with the frozen waters, this was the pre-existing life of the eternal son (Christ Jesus) merging with his lifeless human body on earth for the primary purpose of resurrection. As a pre-existing primordial light, before the Father's expressed utterance in Genesis 1:3, Jesus was and is the eternal son of God. But as the spoken word and expressed light commanded by the Father into physical manifestation (Hebrews 1:1-3), Jesus was and is the resurrected son of God. It is his resurrection from the dead (the revived frozen waters) that began the activities of creation! If Jesus - as the eternal son of the Father, had not appeared in primal beginning (i.e. if his appearance was not facilitated by the 'spoken word' of the Father – which Jesus is.) and the waters were still frozen and dead, nothing could have been created! Jesus would have remained the eternal and unspoken son of God and not revealed to us as the incarnated word of God and the resurrected son of God. Indeed, the spoken word from the Father (John 1:1), the light that is also the word (Psalm 119:130), which began creation **is Christ Jesus.**

As Genesis 1:2-3 unveils, the Father was the light giver; the Spirit was the breath giver and the Son was the manifested light that emitted the warmth of life to the frozen waters (his death), making it possible for the waters to move freely again, and to propagate the formation and creation of life as we know it. Jesus' resurrection began creation, and liquid water existed in our primal beginning because of the resurrection.

John 1:4, continues *'In him [Jesus] was life and the life was the light of men.'* In chemistry, the words of the scripture may read like this: In Jesus was H20 (Water) and in H20 (water) is the hydrogen (light) and oxygen (breathing air) of men. In biology, oxygen is the air that we breathe in, which also sustains our living. In physics, the stars and our sun, which is responsible for daylight and moonlight, are primarily composed of hydrogen.

So that we may contemplate that water did not precede 'the life of Jesus' as it was with Adam and every other earthly creation, the scriptures record that water came out of Jesus' dehydrated body after his death on the cross. The deduction from this text is simply this: Jesus' death gave us life!

John 1:5 states *'And the light shineth in darkness; and the darkness comprehended it not.'* A closer look at John 1:5 suggests that it is not mere light or darkness that's mentioned here. There is a broader context of dialogue that is conceded in this text. Naturally, there can be no communion between light and darkness. When light appears, darkness immediately retreats. However, we are made to feel from this verse that there could be an understanding between the two. Evidently, the biblical text is referring to a personification of light and darkness, which in this instance is Jesus' attempt to communicate and relate to the fallen Adamic race. (Ephesians 5:8 sheds more light on this – **_For ye were sometimes darkness_**, *but now are ye light in the lord: walk as children of light*).

In continuation, John 1:6 states – *There was a man sent from God, whose name was John.* God knew we would not have easily understood his eternal light: the Christ and saviour of the world, so he sent someone before him to help us understand. His name was John, not the John who wrote this Gospel, but another John: the son of Zacharias and Elisabeth, who is often referred to as John the Baptist. John the Baptist was the primary witness of Jesus for one primary reason - Water!! (John 1:31-34)

John 1:7-8 '*The same* [John] *came for a witness, to bear witness of the Light* **that all men** *through him might believe.* ("All men" through John might believe? Selah.) *He* [John] *was not that Light, but was sent to bear witness of that Light.* (In other words, water is the witness of light - Just as we find that water was present at the appearance of the primordial light in Genesis and had preceded its visitation).

John 1:9 - *That was the true Light* [speaking of Jesus], *which lighteth every man that cometh into the world.* [Here again, the scripture confirms that we were the darkness in primordial creation and also implies that we were non-existent in primal beginning, since darkness' existence is by default only: i.e. wherever light is absent. The absence of God from the pre-Adamic race, before our existence, banished the material and immaterial creation of the pre-Adamic world into a state of non-existence. And as we find in Genesis 1:2-12, God made the new earth from the old earth – Psalm 104:30 and we were the darkness called to light].

John 1:10-15: *He* [Jesus] *was in the world, and the world was made by him, and the world knew him not. He came unto his own, and his own received him not. But as many as received him, to them gave he power to become the sons of God,* [this speaks of the church of Jesus, who believes in his deity and embraces the testimony of the resurrection] *even to them that believe on his name: Which were born, not of blood, nor of the will of the flesh, nor of the will of man, but of God* [meaning the church of Jesus was founded from the beginning – Ephesians 1:4]. *And the Word* [Jesus/God] *was made flesh, and dwelt among us, (and we beheld his glory, the glory as of the only begotten of the Father,) full of grace and truth. John* [the Water Baptist] *bare witness of him, and cried, saying, This was*

he of whom I spake, He that cometh after me is preferred before me:
for he was before me. [A new insight is given to us here again.
'Jesus before John' indicates that Jesus is represented by the
water as well as the light].

Though Jesus is the giver of water to all creation, the Father is
the giver of the light [the son] that gave water to all (John
3:16). Water, which is the witness of the incarnated word, is
kept in liquid form by the temperature of heat and warmth
from the sunlight and moonlight, and this is a daily witness to
us of how creation began.

Furthermore, please emphatically note that Jesus did not die
for previous generations, though the primal frozen waters in
Genesis had perished with the pre-Adamic race. What
happened instead is that Jesus gave his sinless life as a mediator
between hades (the present abode of the pre-Adamic race), the
earth and heaven, in order to redeem the spirits and souls of
the fallen Adamic race (See Ephesians 4:9-10).

As shown in the narratives of Genesis 3, the human race
(Adam and Eve) was later deceived by the old serpent (the
Devil) in the Garden of Eden and had become predisposed

(through an inherent knowledge of sin) to follow in the same path as the previous generations of the pre-Adamic era.

Saints who died before the resurrection of Jesus had descended to a region beside hades (Luke 16:22-26), biblically known as Abraham's bosom. These saints of old who were kept in 'the bosom of Abraham' (previously located beside hades) had waited for the coming of Jesus. They knew he would come to take them home from their temporary confinement, but did not know when or how!

In Jesus' first birth as a foetus in the womb of the Virgin Mary, he was God incarnated (Luke 1:31-32). And in his death and burial, he was God incarnated a second time; only this time, he was in hades. This is the reason Revelation 1:5 state that Jesus is *the first begotten of the dead.* And in Revelations 1:18, Jesus said: ***I am he that liveth, and was dead; and, behold, I am alive forevermore, Amen; and have the keys of hell and death.***

While in hades, the divine light from the Father (the first light in Genesis and Son of God) appeared and Jesus' immortal life emerged through his imprisoned human soul and body (i.e. the frozen waters in Genesis and son of man) and the resurrection of the dead became inevitable! The book of Acts

2:24 record that death and hell could no longer hold him captive. Hallelujah!

He died as a son of man because of the temporary separation from the Father at the cross (Matthew 27:46), but was reunited with the promise of the Holy Spirit from the Father (John 14:26, 15:7) while in Hades. He was the first to wait for the promise of the Spirit (the first to experience Pentecost - Acts 1:4-5) and by the Spirit (the Holy Ghost) he resurrected from the dead!

The saints in Hades were also witnesses of Jesus' resurrection power. Before their later ascension into heaven, the scripture record that they appeared unto many in Jerusalem, to show and tell others that they were free from Hades and the grave because of the resurrection of Jesus (Matthew 27:52-53).

Please note that the Biblical depiction of Jesus as the first begotten 'of the dead' (relating to the saints in hades) is slightly different to his depiction as the first born 'from the dead' (relating to earthly sinners who are born partly dead because of the inherent nature of sin from fallen Adam and receive Christ while on earth - Psalms 51:5, Romans 3:23 and 6:23a). Through the resurrection, Jesus emerged as the first born **of** the dead and the first born **from** the dead, and he is also the first born among many brethren, whether dead or alive - Romans 8:29. These subtle variations are important to note because Jesus had brethren in hades before his descent to earth as the child of Joseph and Mary.

Furthermore, our descendent – Adam, did not know God as the resurrection until his death, he only knew God as a creator. After Adam's fall, the primordial darkness in Genesis became apparent and ever since, every human is first born in darkness (metaphorically means without the knowledge of God, Psalm 51:6-7). Then Christ Jesus, who is also known as the last Adam (1 Corinthians 15:45) offered humanity a second birth experience through the power of his resurrection from the dead.

Our first birth as natural beings required spirit (presently mortal breath) and water (Genesis 2:6-7), while the second birth also requires spirit (mortal breath), water, and the resurrection light (Matthew 3:11)! The purpose of the resurrection light is to awaken the human spirit (eternity), which died in humanity since the fall of Adam (Genesis 2:17). Though the human soul is metaphysical and somewhat spiritual, it is not the same as the human spirit. Man (Adam) originally existed in spirit form, in time immemorial as the eternal breath of the almighty: before his existence in an immortal physical form (Genesis 2:7b), which constitutes the soul (mind, emotions, will) and body. After the death of the human spirit (the fall of Adam), the generations of humanity were introduced to earth through the loins of Adam and Eve as offspring of a mortal soul and body with the potential to be so much more!

Adam, who was previously a recipient of the divine breath of God had become like his subordinates (Ecclesiastes 3:19). Other creation also suffered the same fate as Adam because of Adam's disobedience (Genesis 1:26). The original consciousness of the infinite divine is what was lost in the Garden of Eden (Genesis 2:17). However, this loss can be restored to us through an intimate knowledge of Christ Jesus, who is also the last Adam.

The first revelation of God to us in Genesis is as a creator but behind the image of the creator (of our cosmic beginning) is the resurrection. The resurrection of Jesus makes him the creator of the Adamic race. This is one of many reasons we owe our existence to the death and resurrection of Christ Jesus.

Originally, water represented Jesus, but Jesus later shared his life with the Adamic creation by making us a produce of water. The association of water with darkness at the beginning of creation - synonymous with the death of Jesus, represents our first birth (Psalms 18:9-11) and the light that appeared in darkness at the beginning – synonymous with the resurrection of Jesus, was for the purpose of our second birth.

As water, Jesus was easily embraced by darkness i.e. the world of humanity. But as the light, he was often misunderstood (John 1:5). As a carpenter and the son of a woman, Jesus was admired but as soon as he revealed himself to be the son of God, he was despised and rejected (Mark 6:2-3, John 7:11-12). Many preferred and prefer to think of him as a good man and an enlightened teacher but Jesus was so much more than human (John 8:57-58). Through his death on the cross - as in primal beginning, he became the dark waters (Psalm 18:11), and this water was the temporary life for the darkness - which we were, before we believed. His death gave us natural life, just as we find water and blood streamed from his lifeless body at the cross (John 19:34). We were the darkness, he was the water, together we became the dark waters and this frozen dark waters (at the beginning) represented Jesus (on the cross) and the Adamic race. Today, we are water composites because he was first water.

Jesus identified with the world of humanity through his death on the cross, but the world is also given the opportunity to identify with him by believing in the testimony of his resurrection from the dead for their sake. (Without this demonstration of faith, we cannot please God - Hebrews 11:6) The death and resurrection of Jesus has been confirmed by several reliable historians: Jews, Romans, and Greek historians who were not even disciples of Jesus. It is an authentic verifiable historicity and cannot be trivialised or ignored if we intend that God takes us seriously. It was personal to God and still is. It was the death of his son for our salvation and recreation - 2 Corinthians 5:17.

A privileged eternal life is promised to us through Jesus only (John 17:3) and just as Jesus (and the scriptures before his human conception) had predicted his death and resurrection, so will all who believe in Jesus die and resurrect to inherit a privileged eternal life (John 1:12).

Please note that the resurrection of Jesus is nothing like that of Lazarus or those who had been miraculously raised from the dead before him. The others returned to die again but Jesus' resurrection was final and eternal. Jesus provided a compelling evidence for heaven and showed us the proof of eternal life by resurrecting from the dead and living among humans after his death (Luke 24:36-48). The sublime message of his resurrection was simply this: "there is life after death", and furthermore, only the life and teachings of Jesus can be trusted in matters relating to eternity. No other founder of a religion conquered the grave, not even the first Adam. Jesus personally announced in John 11:25-26: '*...I am the resurrection, and the life: he that believeth in me, though he were dead, yet shall he live: And whosoever liveth and believeth in me shall never die* [meaning their death can only lead to a glorious resurrection]. *Believest thou this?*

ENCORE: WHY WATER?

Why is the earth and the human body mostly water?

Think about it... if God had a son and began the creation of the world with a son, beside sending messengers to us to tell us of his son, and sending even his own son, how else can he help us perceive and understand this divine truth? Water!! He puts water in everything and everywhere. God began the world with water: symbolic of having a child or son, to reveal to us that he was first a Father before his emerging identity as a creator.

During the baptism of Jesus, the Father spoke audibly from the skies as Jesus was pulled out of water by John the Baptist – openly affirming the baptism of Jesus as a birthing experience, he announced: *This is my beloved 'son' in whom I am well pleased* (Matthew 3:16). On this occasion, the Spirit was not the only eye witness, John and the people who were present at the baptism of Jesus were also eye witnesses. These words were publicly expressed by the Father at the time not only to express his love for the Son but to also reveal a truth that we can all relate to: the birth of a child is inextricably linked with being drawn out of water. Isaiah 9:6 declares *'For unto us a child is born, unto us a son is given: and the government shall be upon his shoulder: and his name shall be called Wonderful, Counselor, The mighty God, The everlasting Father, The Prince of Peace.'*

After the Holy Ghost fell on Jesus (in the apparition of a dove), during his water baptism, light also fell on him (similar to the scenery in Genesis when light appeared in darkness). Then, for the first time **in public**, the Father revealed the identity of the son to John and the world of humanity (Selah). Do you know what truth sounds like when you hear it? Truth is a rare commodity and those who tell it are endangered species.

Genesis 1:2: ***And the earth was without form and void; and darkness was upon the face of the deep. And the spirit of God moved upon the face of the waters. And God said let there be light...***

It's easy to forget that we lived in the dark for the first nine to ten months of our human existence, enveloped in the deep dark shadow of a womb, surrounded by pro-creation waters, and the first thing we saw after nine to ten months of several nights was light! Simultaneously, with that light, we saw blood!! (1John 1:7 and 1 John 5:7-8)

To recap the above chapter, please view Table 1 below

Table 1 – Genesis 1:2-3

Literal Text	Biblical Meaning
1. The Deep	Hades - the abysmal pit of fallen angels and demons
2. Surface of the Deep	Ocean deep, graves and buried pre-adamic fossils
3. Darkness	Fallen human race since the fall of Adam
4. Primordial Water	Son of man, born sinless, like the original Adam (Jesus)
5. The Spirit of God	The Breath of life and Holy Ghost
6. Primordial Light	The Incarnated Word, The Light and Son of God (Christ)
7. Primordial Voice	The Father - Orator of The Word and Giver of The Light

Finally, let's hear directly from God himself.

GOD SPEAKS

_____

The book of Job 38

¹Then the LORD answered Job out of the whirlwind, and said,

²Who is this that darkeneth counsel by words without knowledge?

³Gird up now thy loins like a man; for I will demand of thee, and answer thou me.

⁴Where wast thou when I laid the foundations of the earth? declare, if thou hast understanding.

⁵Who hath laid the measures thereof, if thou knowest? or who hath stretched the line upon it?

⁶Whereupon are the foundations thereof fastened? [Symbolic of the pillars of the church: the Apostles and Prophets, who are types of the Apostle Peter – Matthew16:18] or who laid the corner stone thereof; [Symbolic of Christ Jesus, the first founding pillar and head of the church – Ephesians 2:20]

⁷When the morning stars sang together, and all the sons of God shouted for joy? [These were angels, the immortal children of God – Psalms 89:6 and Luke 20:36]

^{8} Or who shut up the sea with doors [The frozen waters in Genesis], when it brake forth, as if it had issued out of the womb? [A comparison to the water-break of a pregnant woman before child birth, just as Jesus was born from the dead at the beginning]

^{16} Hast thou entered into the springs of the sea? or hast thou walked in the search of the depth? [This speaks of underneath the sea, where the surface of the deep and the deep is located.]

^{17} Have the gates of death been opened unto thee? or hast thou seen the doors of the shadow of death? [This again speaks of the surface of the deep and the deep, its entry and exit gates, which consist of the pre-Adamic fossils and the buried fossils in the days of Noah. In addition, far below it, is the abysmal residence of demonic spirits and fallen angels. Jesus also makes mention of this in Matthew 16:18, when he spoke of 'the gates of hell' that seek to prevail against the foundation of the church – i.e. 'Himself', and his church family, which was pre-elected in him from the foundation of the world']

¹⁸ Hast thou perceived the breadth of the earth? declare if thou knowest it all.

¹⁹ Where is the way where light dwelleth? and as for darkness, where is the place thereof [Where did Light come from? The primordial light that engendered all other lights, where is its origin? And as for darkness, it does not exist, except in the absence of light]

²⁰ That thou shouldest take it to the bound thereof, and that thou shouldest know the paths to the house thereof? [Can you find where Heaven is, from bands and circles of lights? Can you measure the distance to Heaven from the stars?]

²¹ Knowest thou it, because thou wast then born? or because the number of thy days is great? [How can you know these things? How can you understand these things? You are but a created being and your days are numbered]

²⁴ By what way is the light parted, which scattereth the east wind upon the earth? [This speaks of the first appearance of the

primordial light in Genesis 1:3, which was preceded by the towering wind of the Spirit in Genesis 1:2]

²⁵ Who hath divided a watercourse for the overflowing of waters, [This speaks of the breaking and melting of the frozen waters by the strong wind of the Spirit and the permeating heat from the brilliance of the primordial Light] or a way for the lightning of thunder; [This speaks of the open sky and open heaven for the fall of rain]

²⁶ To cause it to rain on the earth, where no man is; on the wilderness, wherein there is no man; [Where were you when it first rained on the barren earth?]

²⁷ To satisfy the desolate and waste ground; and to cause the bud of the tender herb to spring forth? [Where were you when vegetation was engendered by the first rain?]

²⁸ Hath the rain a father? or who hath begotten the drops of dew? [Though water may appear in the form of rain and dew, and as part

of creation, it is somewhat without a parental origin and does not share the same creative history as the others.]

²⁹ Out of whose **womb** came the ice? and the hoary frost of heaven [!], who hath gendered it? [Water has no extrinsic created origin in the narratives of Genesis because it is a witness of the unnatural son of man and uncreated son of God. Though water is created, it was not spoken into existence like the other creation in Genesis]

³⁰ The waters are hid as with a stone, and the face of the deep is frozen. [Genesis 1:2 – Look and consider, the waters were already present before creation. My son was slain from the foundation of your world!]

BEFORE AND AFTER

Isn't London English and rain wet? Isn't summer hot and winter cold? Try as we may to redefine the obvious, the definition of God can never change - without a beginning and without end - this is God. This is God.

Every now and again, I meet individuals who refer to themselves as GOD. Ironically, these individuals do not believe that God exists. Evidently, they have heard this from someone who pretends to be non-religious. I know what they are trying to say – they are referring to themselves as the universe because they think the universe represents "the ultimate reality" and has created itself. But if we really understood the transient nature of our universe, we would not even associate with this pretence.

Evidences for a finite universe were supplied in the 1920's, when a scientist by the name of Edward Hubble discovered that the universe must have been smaller and denser at earlier points in its history. This startling discovery confirmed the biblical perspective of a transient and temporary universe. If we choose to view ourselves as mere extensions of the universe, then we have also chosen to inhibit and restrain our infinite potential to the finality of a finite future.

The answer God gave to Moses when asked who he was revealed what it takes to be God. 'I AM THAT I AM' that's what God said about himself to Moses, which means that God is "independent" and self-existent. To be independent is something humans seldom understand. In the real context of its meaning, independence suggests that a person should rely 'solely-inwardly' for his or her survival and care. An actual "independent" being would need no breathing air from his or her external surroundings. He or she would not depend on food, shelter, clothing or anything whatsoever from the external to survive. Such a person should be self-existing. Certainly, no living human of this kind exists. It is words like *independence* that have lured and encouraged the human mind to create an inflated sense of self-pride and egotistical beliefs that dismiss the need for a supreme creator. Only God is realistically independent. We are not independent whether in spirit, soul or body.

The same truism that is applicable to *independence* applies to the attributes of being *a creator* like God. Humans are not original creators (though sometimes authentic). To be original in creating will necessitate the use of our body parts to create the world around us. What we create is from what is already created, that is, within nature, and all of nature was created by a creator other than human. Even our creative ideas are often derived from nature. E.g. Airplanes (man-made) are imitations of birds (God-made). It is self-defeating to think that a finite universe could have created itself or to think that something which ultimately exists as a final and first cause created itself (Selah). The Bible maintains that God is uncreated. This is why he is the supreme creator.

If creation had been formed from God's innate self, we would have not been able to distinguish the created from the creator, but because creation was formed extrinsically, is the reason we have a temporal universe (Matthew 24:35).

God is the only thing that's invariably permanent among creation. The mystery of Genesis is not that God created something out of nothing but that he created a state of nothingness so that creation could originate with a beginning. Without a definite nothingness, nothing would have appeared created. It is because of the created nothingness that the heavens and the earth exist with an actual beginning, hence the reason for Genesis 1:1 'In the beginning, God created the heavens and the earth'. There would have been no real beginning except there was a pre-existent state of nothingness and this pre-existing nothing was also created. There has never been '*nothing*' until God created it. Instead, there has always been something - the ultimate something that created every thing and that something is someone, whom we refer to as God.

The opening words of Genesis 1:1 '*In the beginning...*' implicitly reveal that God paused to create *nothing* in order to create something else.

Naturally, the only way to create nothingness from something that is self-existing would be to destroy the only thing that exists. In which case, it would have been utterly impossible to create anything whatsoever. However, the miracle of creation was possible to achieve because God is supernatural. Nothing should ever produce something but nothing actually went on to produce something because there was someone supernatural behind that nothing. Certainly, *absolute nothing cannot produce anything whatsoever but a created nothing could*. These are some of the things that have baffled the scientific community. The astronomical narrative of the universe makes sense yet it doesn't. Albert Einstein puts this brilliantly: *'The most unintelligible thing about the universe is that it is intelligible at all.'* Creation must have come out of something yet it seems like nothing is beneath it all.

The existence of a state of nothingness at the heart of our cosmic origin is a mind-boggling illusion that has brought scientific atheism to its knees. When is all said and done, no gods can stand before the Creator. The universe is riddled with his mischievous scheme, so that if we cannot see the creator's hand, we can acknowledge his handiwork. Subsequently, many adherents of scientific atheism are restricted to support the view that **absolute nothing** lies behind the existence of our universe knowing fully well that this view contradicts their natural reasoning and logic. The truism of the words of a song from 'Sound Of Music' serenades the cosmic sea of space and galaxies *'nothing comes from nothing, nothing ever could.'* In other words, to understand the universe, we have to believe in the existence of God.

The quest to understand the universe lies within the scope of the human heart. The battle for the mind is already won. The divine creator has no cause to exist other than himself, for he is divine. However, the universe needs a divine creator for its existence. The scriptures reveal the persons of the divine as the Father, Son and Holy Ghost – also known as the Holy Trinity.

Because God existed before creation, the only possible way to describe God to creation is to use something that's created. We cannot easily recognise God as we would each other. Even if we saw God walking down the street, it's possible not to recognise him. Besides creation, God is theoretically indescribable, and because God existed before creation, he is altogether indescribable, except he is revealed to us. I like the way Bishop Noel Jones puts this, he said: 'God is everywhere but nowhere if you don't meet him somewhere'.

Every human that encounters God can only recognise God through a vehicle of revelation. Jacob and Joshua saw him in the likeness and image of an angel. Abraham met God as three travelling strangers. Moses heard the voice of God in the midst of a celestial fire that did not burn. Paul saw him as a light from heaven. John the Baptist saw him in the apparition of a dove in the sky and a man in water. Peter, James and John saw him as a Jewish rabbi who had come from heaven. The Pharisees and Sadducees saw him as the son of a carpenter and a blasphemer. Mary saw him as the virgin child of her womb, and at a gathering of many eye witnesses in the river Jordan,

God disclosed his identity as a Father when he announced from heaven that Jesus was his son (Mark 1:9-11). We cannot know God any other way but by revelation because we have never seen the fullness of God before! Since the beginning of creation until now, God has always taken lesser forms to relate to creation. This is why it should come as no surprise to find that God came to earth in the image and form of a man, named Jesus Christ.

Afterall, God (in his foreknowledge) had originally created humans in his image and likeness – Genesis 1:26. In John 1:1-14, the scriptures confirm that Jesus was present at the beginning of creation as a co-creator and had manifested in human flesh to identify with humans and reconcile us to an intimate communion and fellowship with God.

In John 17:5, Jesus prayed the following: *'And now, O **Father**, glorify thou me with thine own self with the glory which I had with thee before the world was.'* Evidently, Jesus admitted to an exclusive relationship with the Father before creation. His prayers reveal that God has a pre-existing identity, and that both the previous, present and future identities of God encapsulate God's fullness.

245

Creation can only see God through the microscopic lens of itself as a creature but cannot see God in full. This is because God exists more fully than any of his creation. To assume that God solely exists externally is incomplete. God is not merely an independent existence but the fullness of existence. Acts 17:28 records *'For in him we live, and move, and have our being...'*

God can be both temporary (time) and eternal (timeless) and is neither imprisoned by his timelessness nor time. His temporary existence made the creation of a finite universe possible and his eternal existence makes him the infinite divine. He is absolutely and creatively free, and if he wasn't as free, he would not be God.

While it is that we enjoy partial freedom as partial expressions of God, God also enjoys absolute freedom as the divine. However, he expresses his absolute freedom by employing the provision of any one of his created laws to negate the limitation and restriction of another. He is law abiding even when indulging his inherent privileges as an absolute free being. He is a God that leads by example. This is one of many reasons that God came in the model of his own creation, in the person of Christ Jesus, to show us the integrity and truth that he possesses by keeping the very same laws that he once asked his creation to observe. Jesus also suffered and died as creation has. He fulfilled every law of the Old Testament on our behalf and those who honour the life and teachings of Jesus have kept the commandments of God (Matthew 5:17). Furthermore, because God predates the laws that he made for creation, God can choose to be sovereign if necessary and has every justifiable right to do so.

In the life of Jesus, who was both God and man, God sovereignly expressed his creative freedom by combining both his infinite nature and the finite nature of creation in the person of Christ Jesus (who was God incarnated).

Until Jesus came, the descendants of Adam had not cohabitated with God (John 14:7). Even Jacob who thought he saw the face of God had only glimpsed a revelation of God in the pulchritude of a passing angel. His encounter with God was for a fleeting moment. No man can see God fully on earth except the incarnated son of God; and even in heaven, the angels cannot see God's full glory because they are also created entities. God is higher and above the heavens and the earth (Psalm 113:4). He is distant from us even when closest to us. The book of Psalms 139:5-10 narrates this intriguing exposition – *'Thou hast beset me behind and before, and laid thine hand upon me. Such knowledge is too wonderful for me; it is high, I cannot attain unto it. Whither shall I go from thy spirit? Or whither shall I flee from thy presence? If I ascend up into heaven, thou art there: if I make my bed in hell, behold, thou art there. If I take the wings of the morning, and dwell in the uttermost parts of the sea; Even there shall thy hand lead me, and thy right hand shall hold me.'*

No created being could possibly contain all the limitless and boundless heights, breadths, lengths and depths of the creator God. God has no home but in himself, he has made himself smaller so that heaven can contain him. Though he dwells in heaven, yet eternity exists in him (John 17:3).

Isaiah 66:1-2 reveals *'Thus saith the Lord, The heaven is my throne, and the earth is my footstool: where is the house that ye build unto me? And where is the place of my rest? For all those things hath mine hand made, and all those things have been* [meaning all creation exists in him], *saith the Lord...'* Virtue from God's pre-existing and pre-creation glory have dispersed to his works of creation, yet God as the infinite divine is not fragmented because he is not a thing but a being. All things created belong to God, yet God exists independently. All things created are God's but not God (!) because God already existed before creation.

In heaven, the greatest revelation of God to creation is the Father (Matthew 6:9). On earth, the greatest revelation of God to creation is the Son - Jesus (John 3:16) and in between and all around is the Holy Spirit (Psalm 139:5-10).

John 1:18 states *'No man hath seen God at anytime* [meaning it is not possible to see God in his fullness within the boundaries of time]*;* [except] *the only begotten son, which is in the bosom of the Father* [Jesus who emerged from the divine] *he hath declared him* [To 'declare' in oxford dictionary means to 'make clear', to 'reveal one's identity' and to 'formally announce the beginning of...']. This text reveals that we cannot see God clearly except through Jesus.

Matthew 11:27 sheds more light *'All things are delivered to me of my Father* [Jesus speaking]*: and* **no man knoweth the Son, but the Father; neither knoweth any man the Father, save the Son, and** *he* **to whomsoever the Son will reveal** *him.'* Here again, this text explicitly expressed that the Father is neither revealed to the Son nor the Son revealed to the Father, but both are revealed only to creation. Evidently, it is not necessary for both to be revealed to each other because they are co-creators of creation and know each other well. Additionally, Jesus confirms that it is not only the Father that cannot be directly known to men but that he, as well, cannot be directly known to men (except the Father reveals him).

In a later text in Matthew 16:13-17, this is exactly what happened. After Jesus asked his disciples who the people thought he was, and who they think he is. The disciple Peter gave the right answer but Jesus said to Peter that this answer was not his own but had come from the Father.

'When Jesus came into the coasts of Caesarea Philippi, he asked his disciples, saying, Whom do men say that I the Son of man am? And they said, Some say that thou art John the Baptist: some, Elias; and others, Jeremias, or one of the prophets. He saith unto them, But whom say ye that I am? And Simon Peter answered and said, Thou art the Christ, the Son of the living God. And Jesus answered and said unto him, Blessed art thou, Simon Barjona: for flesh and blood hath not revealed it unto thee, but my Father who is in heaven.'

It follows then, that much like the Father, Jesus, the Son of God is a revelation to creation. Beyond our furthest imaginations and distant thoughts, beyond our doubts and beliefs, between our heart and soul and a world devoid of pretence, God is everything that's everything that contains everything there is. He is God and incomparable!

When I look up to heaven, I think of his transcendent nature, when I look down within me, I think of his immanent spirit.

250

He is within and without me, before and after all that is, all that was and all that ever will be.

EVERYTHING

In seeking God, we find everything else. Everything can be explained.

Q&A

Why has the Holy Trinity been difficult to understand until now?

The reason for this is anthropomorphology, which basically means using what is known to explain the unknown and using the things we understand to explain the things we barely understand. As a result of this methodical approach in theology and science, many finite models and concepts have been employed to explain the triune God, who is infinite! Though many of these models have proven inadequate in explaining the intrinsic architecture of the Godhead (The Holy Trinity), they have helped to illustrate the differences in their functions and manifestations but not their persons. However, God, in his infinite knowledge, had preordained that the sun, moon and stars (three celestial bodies of light) would serve as the commissioned and authorised symbols to convey the intricacies and interrelations of the differences, similarities, and uniqueness of each personality in the Holy Trinity. Furthermore, other examples and models of the trinity here on earth can be easily manipulated and altered by human hands, but the sun, moon and stars cannot be easily exploited! While other models may serve as hints and traces of the triune God, including our planet earth (which is the third planet from the sun), the sun, moon and stars are the signs and signature of the Holy Trinity.

What is the Biblical significance and meaning of the Holy Trinity?

The doctrine of the Holy Trinity is the canopy of the gospel of Christ, commissioned by our Lord Jesus (after his resurrection) to the first apostles of the gospel and his church, and for all nations of people on planet earth (Matthew 28:19). The Holy Trinity consists of three distinct persons, who are not the same as the other, yet are the same God. The Father is not the Son, the Son is not the Holy Spirit, and the Holy Spirit is not the Father, yet all three are co-eternal and co-exist as one triune deity!

Is the Godhead the same as the Holy Trinity?

The biblical term 'Godhead' is used thrice in the scriptures – Selah (meaning pause and think). In Romans 1:20, the Godhead was a reference for the Father and Son (while the eternal power represented the Holy Spirit in this chapter and verse). In Colossians 2:9, the Godhead was a reference for the Son, and in Acts 17:29, the Godhead was a reference for all three members of the trinity.

How is it possible that God is one and three distinct persons, but not three Gods?

The solution to this conundrum is hidden in one word (perhaps three) that best describes God and is compatible with the Bible and modern science. God is a Government! The befitting acronym for God (in English) is simply this: Government Of Divinity or Government Of Deity.

When we look around, what do we find? Laws, **Universal Laws**! And most certainly, there can be no laws without a lawgiver or government. The universe could not have existed without laws. It is from nature that all scientific laws are derived. It was the law of gravity that pulled matter together so that planets, stars and other complex organisms could be formed. There are laws everywhere! To name a few: motion, reproduction, gravity, thermodynamics and relativity. The principle of law permeates the cosmos and is also expressed in the human conscience and human society. No person will rule a nation of free wills and different personalities without implementing a system of government. No persons would manage a large territorial space of moving and living creatures without implementing an administrative system of government. The universe could not have continued to exist without its universal laws! It is a government that created the universe and that government (also known as God) was established by three persons, namely 'The Father', 'The Son' and 'The Holy Ghost'. *(We shall find the intricacies of this divine government in Volume 6)*

Can the Bible be trusted?

Yes.

A preacher by the name of Gregory Dickow realised the ministry of Jesus began with *three* words and ended with *three* words: *"It is written"* and *"It is finished"*. This is because that which is written by the moving fingers of God (the Holy Spirit) cannot be unwritten. God is an author and the best writer there is. He has authored several books, some of which are: 'The Book of Remembrance' – Malachi 3:16, 'The Book of Life' - Revelations 20:12, and of course, the Bible.

TELL THEM I LOVE THEM...

*'Though I speak with the tongues of men and of angels, and have not charity [**love**], I am become as sounding brass, or a tinkling cymbal.*

*And though I have the gift of prophecy, and understand all mysteries, and all knowledge; and though I have all faith, so that I could remove mountains, and have not charity [**love**], I am nothing.*

*And though I bestow all my goods to feed the poor, and though I give my body to be burned, and have not charity [**love**], it profiteth me nothing.'*

~ 1 Corinthians 13:1-3

What is love? Who is love?

In faith, we may differ

But in love, we are related

For even those who do not believe

Jesus died for you.

'And [pray] for me, that utterance may be given unto me, that I may open my mouth boldly, to make known **the mystery** of the gospel, For which I am an **ambassador** in bonds: that therein I may speak boldly, as I ought to speak.'

~ Ephesians 6:19–20

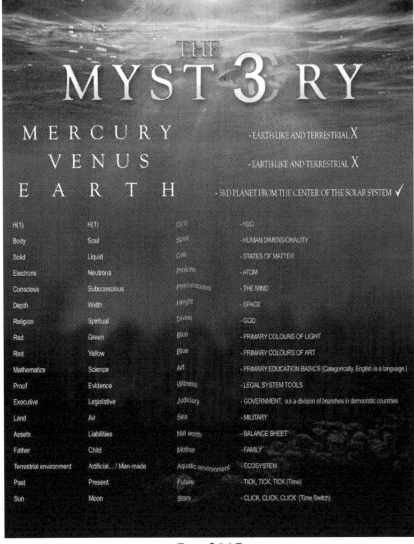

Out 2015

EXCERPTS FROM THE MYSTERY:

MIND THE GAPS

The mathematical language we find in the substratum of the universe that helps the human mind to contemplate and understand the undertruths of the universe was intellectually devised by the cognitive ability of a mindful creator who intends to relate to his creation. God is a being and not a thing and mind does not come from matter but matter from mind. So please mind the gaps.

God may read like poetry but he is non-fiction. His primordial voice has not grown silent since creation began; his echo still travels through the cosmic sea, defying gravity and every known law of physics. **What is dark matter and dark energy?** Planet scientists realise what it's not but they cannot tell us what it is…

A TRUTH AS BIG AS GOD

A truth as big as God cannot be hidden, even in the depths of the night, it cannot lie.

Until Jesus came, we could not ascertain that God was a person. The incarnation of God in human flesh cannot be trivialised if we believe that God is a person and not some "thing". Long before the birth of Christ, Isaiah 7:14 announced: ... **The Lord <u>himself</u>** *shall give you a sign; Behold a virgin shall conceive and bear a son, and shall call his name Immanuel* (Meaning God with us).

A few years ago, I was awakened by the most fascinating realisation: It is not that Jesus Christ is the absolute truth but rather, the absolute truth is Jesus Christ. The religiosity of Christianity had taught me the former but when God finally revealed himself to me, I realised the latter. I was able to find

God in everything and almost anywhere because a truth as big as God cannot be hidden.

This is the reason that some of what we find in the Bible can be identified in other religious creeds and texts. This is also the reason that some of what may seem opposed to the Bible in other religions may somehow correlate with the mysteries of the Bible to reveal an underlying unity - a truth as big as God cannot be hidden! Some Bible theologians have dubbed these frequent correlations an objective proportional revelation. They express that truths in the Bible can be found in many religions, however, the Bible is fundamentally different to any other book or religion. For example, just because we can find the colour yellow in green does not make green yellow (blue + yellow = green. So green - yellow = blue).

There is a difference between a partial truth and a whole truth. Sadly, a partial truth will often imply that it is also partly false. In fact, most clever lies consist of partial truths. Our quest to establish the absolute truth about God, life and death does not mean we have to know everything about everything to ascertain that it is wholly true. However, it is important that we are certain of what we think we know, because it's possible to be sincerely wrong. It is possible to know more than we understand. This is the burden that all human must carry; this is the quest that all humanity must confront and face. Absolute truth is a rare commodity and can cost us everything. We must learn to think for ourselves and not let others think for us. We must learn to seek God with all our hearts. We must ask ourselves why we believe what we believe and to what end is our faith. What proof is there? What kind of tangible evidence exists for our beliefs? What is the article and constitution of our faith? What answers do we find in there? What have we personally experienced? What do we really know and what don't we know for certain? Why do we truly believe what we believe? Is it tradition or much more? Is it liberating and fulfilling? Is it full of truth, love and life? Is it substantial or unsubstantiated? Is it cosmic and authentic? Is it objective and subjective? Is it human or divine? ...

IF IT IS MATTER, IT SHOULD MATTER

If it looks like a duck, walks like a duck, feeds like a duck, mates like a duck, sleeps like a duck, fights like a duck, waddles like a duck and swims like a duck. Honey, please, it is a duck.

It is fascinating (though unsurprising) that the Qur'an agrees with the Bible on the subject of water. Recorded in Sura 21 The Prophets, ayat 30, the Qur'an states: *"We have made every living thing out of water."*

Beside the use of *We* in reference to Allah in this text, it will be intellectually dishonest to presume that God created and formed every living thing out of water and not seriously consider the concept of trinity as the alpha of all creation.

There is nothing more elusive than the obvious because the obvious is too close to miss yet easy to ignore and dismiss.

While it is that water appears as one singular entity, it is also

265

important to note that water consists of *three* molecule gases. With the contribution of modern science, we have now discovered that the water we think we know and can see with our naked eyes stands on the sub of H20 – meaning two hydrogen gas molecules and one oxygen gas molecule are the substance that makes up water – they are the undercurrent and underlying structure and architecture of water. And if at anytime, one or two gas molecules went missing, then water as we know it could not have been or can ever be! (Selah).

In addition, planet scientists have confirmed in recent years that the water in the human body is older than the planet itself. So it appears that no other religion or the non religious are excluded from the proposition on the subject of water and creation...

CREDIT AND REFERENCE NOTES

I would like to express my gratitude to Wikipedia and the National Geographic Channel for the information that I was able to acquire from them to help conduct my research while writing this book. Thank you so very much.

Professor Edgar H. Andrews, Who Made God Pg 90 – Publisher EP Books 2009

ACKNOWLEDGEMENTS

I would like to express my deepest gratitude to the many people who saw me through this book, especially to those who have endured my mental and emotional absence.

To Pastor Jennifer, my spiritual matron and friend: thank you for always believing in me, for accepting me, for your prayers, your unswerving love, humility, wisdom and words of encouragement. My walk with God has been so enriched by your life and example. You have contributed immensely to finding my voice and identity in the global church.

To Dr Brown, thank you for your mentorship and your belief in me. It's been so long since I've seen you but I still carry you in my heart.

To my Father and my sisters, I love you all so much and hope I make you proud.

To Dele Raheem: God knew I would not have had enough sense to choose you as a friend so he chose you instead for me. Thank you for always challenging me and correcting me. Thank you for always believing in me, and for our friendship and brotherhood. Your commitment to our friendship has propelled this book project to great heights and feats that ordinary men would not dare. You are extraordinary and I thank God for you always.

To Katarina H Raheem: Thank you for your comments and editorial inputs, for your readiness to assist whenever I call and for your kind and enamouring spirit. You are a beautiful soul and I'm so glad God sent you my way.

To Temi Oyewole, thank you for your editorial contribution and tireless labour to meet our nearly impossible deadlines. Your enthusiasm and belief in this project has been so encouraging and liberating. You are truly God sent.

To my ace and champion – Isaac Sanya, I'm always so proud of you and so humbled to have you as a brother. Your critiques, insights and expertise have enhanced this book immensely. I don't think I would have been able to write this book without your help. Thank you so very much for your sacrifices and patience when I felt handicapped. I love you so dearly.

To Emmanuel Garuba: Thank you for leading me to the Lord Jesus when I was only nine. For showing me the way and for seeing in me what I could not see in myself even then. You will always be a part of my heart. What you sowed in me, you gave to everyone I've ever loved and touched. God remembers and I do too.

To Bunmi Oladipo: You are a friend among friends, irreplaceable and indispensable, thank you for always being there. You are a man after my own heart, authentic and genuine. I will always be your brother and friend.

To my Mother: I know you don't think you've given me much but you've given me everything I could ever ask for. For your patience and forgiveness, I thank you. For your compassion and care, I thank you. For your kindness and empathy, I thank you. For always respecting my calling and recognising my purpose for existing since I could remember, thank you. You are the kindest woman I know and I will be fortunate to meet a woman half as kind as you. If I had to choose, I could not have chosen a better mother. Thank you for always trying when all others would have given up. You are a tough lover and I'm thankful to God that you are my mother.

To the Holy Spirit, I only wish the world will know how real you are. I don't intend to separate you from my family and friends. You should know this but I'll like to tell you anyway. You are the greatest teacher and friend I know, and I'm crazy about you. Xxx

Printed in Great Britain
by Amazon

34494771R00155